5.00

D0114290

NO LONGER PROPERTY OF
BRESCIA COLLEGE LIBRARY

15.00

CELTIC
F·I·R·E

CELTIC
F·I·R·E

The Passionate
Religious Vision of
Ancient Britain and Ireland

◆ ◆ ◆

EDITED BY ROBERT
VAN DE WEYER

◆

DOUBLEDAY
NEW YORK   LONDON   TORONTO   SYDNEY
AUCKLAND

BRESCIA COLLEGE LIBRARY
OWENSBORO, KENTUCKY

PUBLISHED BY DOUBLEDAY
a division of Bantam Doubleday Dell
Publishing Group, Inc.
666 Fifth Avenue, New York, New York 10103

DOUBLEDAY and the portrayal of an anchor with a dolphin
are trademarks of Doubleday, a division of Bantam
Doubleday Dell Publishing Group, Inc.

Originally published in Great Britain by Darton, Longman
and Todd, Ltd.

Book design by Jessica Shatan

Library of Congress Cataloging-in-Publication Data
Celtic fire : the passionate religious vision of ancient Britain
and Ireland / edited by Robert Van de Weyer.—1st ed.
    p.   cm.
Translated from Celtic.
Includes bibliographical references.
1. Christian literature, Celtic.
I. Van de Weyer, Robert.
BP53.C35   1991
274.1'03—dc20   90-24094 CIP

ISBN 0-385-41958-9

274
.103
C394

Copyright © 1990 by Robert Van de Weyer

All Rights Reserved

Printed in the United States of America

September 1991

1   3   5   7   9   10   8   6   4   2

First Edition in the United States of America

BERSEA COLLEGE LIBRARY
OWENSBORO, KENTUCKY

CONTENTS

INTRODUCTION	1
The Confession of Patrick	27
Brigid's City	36
The Voyage of Brendan	43
Columba's Island	59
Aidan and Oswald	73
Cuthbert's Kingdom	81
Hilda and Caedmon	96
Iltut's School	103
Saints and Beasts	113
Monks and Hermits	124
Scribes and Scholars	138
Prayers Through the Day	143
Prayers for Protection	148
Prayers of Life and Death	154
Songs to Jesus	160
God and the Soul	170
Riches and Poverty	179
The Celtic Psalter	189
The Four Seasons	195
The Encounters of Moling	200

◆　◆　◆

◆

85897

The Vision of Seth   205
Gnomic Poems   209
Triads   218
A Celtic Pilgrimage   221
BIBLIOGRAPHY   246

CELTIC
F·I·R·E

CELTIC FIRE

INTRODUCTION

In every church and monastery of Celtic Britain and Ireland a fire was kept burning, day and night, summer and winter, as a sign of God's presence. And at Kildare, the site of Brigid's great convent, the fire was sustained for a further thousand years, as a memorial both of the saint herself, and of that passionate Christian devotion which burst into flame in these remote islands between the fifth and seventh centuries. While the rest of Europe was entering a dark age of conflict and division, after the fall of the Roman Empire, the Christian gospel was lighting the hearts of the rugged Celtic tribesmen; and thousands upon thousands of simple men and women became

* * *

monks and missionaries, poets and pilgrims, ablaze with the love of Christ.

Today in the late twentieth century the Celtic fire is burning anew. As the scale of our ecological crisis becomes apparent, men and women are seeking a spirituality which embraces the natural order, kindling our love for the animals and birds, trees and insects with whom we share this fragile planet. The Catholic and Protestant traditions are often indifferent, even hostile to nature, treating her as irrelevant to our spiritual salvation, or even as a source of corruption. There are, of course, shining exceptions, such as Francis of Assisi and Mother Julian whose works are again immensely popular. But in Celtic Christianity we have an entire church which saw within every living creature the divine spirit, and so loved all creatures for their own sake. Thus the Celts offer a spirituality for our time.

◆   ◆   ◆

The Celtic fire had three main sources. The first was the ancient Druid religion. There are

◆   ◆   ◆

◆

numerous accounts of Christian evangelists in direct contest with Druid priests, vying to see whose miraculous powers were greatest; indeed the climaxes of Patrick's mission to Ireland, and of Columba's mission to the Picts, were such battles in the presence of powerful kings and chiefs. But far from rejecting their old religion, the Christian Celts continued to hold it in the deepest respect, absorbing many of its ideas and attitudes, symbols and rituals, into their new faith. Druidic philosophy placed great emphasis on love and on forgiving the wrongs of others, and taught that those who were loving and merciful on this earth would receive eternal bliss. So conversion to Christianity involved no change in moral belief. More striking, however, were the role of women and the pattern of ministry. The Druid priesthood included both men and women, enjoying equal status; and this was maintained in the Celtic church, in which, contrary to the practice in the rest of Christendom, women frequently ruled great churches and monasteries frequently con-

◆   ◆   ◆

◆

tained both men and women, with a woman in charge, such as Kildare under Brigid and Whitby under Hilda. In addition to the priesthood the Druids had an order of "filid," wandering poets and prophets who taught religion to the common people. The Celtic church adopted this ministry with enthusiasm. Men and women were actually ordained to the office of "bard," authorised to convey the Christian gospel in simple ballads and songs. And there were numerous "pilgrims," monks and nuns who travelled by land and sea wherever the Spirit led them, carrying the gospel to the remotest regions and lands, even as far as America.

The second major influence on Celtic Christianity was the desert fathers of Egypt. Stories of these first Christian monks, and their wise and witty sayings, were collected together, and enjoyed huge popularity throughout the Mediterranean. Copies were brought by traders as far west as Britain and Ireland, instantly capturing the Celtic imagination. The quirky humour of the desert monks, their stubborn

* * *

individualism, and, above all, their love of nature appealed to the Celtic spirit, greatly enhancing the attraction of the Christian faith. And within a few decades of the first Christian mission, the Celts were establishing monasteries of their own, which became the spiritual and cultural heart of the Celtic church. Despite the efforts of Patrick and others influenced by Roman ideas, the political structure of the continental church, based on the major cities and towns, could never function in a land of scattered farms and hilltop fortresses. The monasteries, by contrast, created a new Christian society, which people could visit and observe, and where they could gather for worship. Thus the abbots and abbesses became the local religious leaders, and their communities the means through which Christian ideas infused the tribal culture.

The third main influence was the doctrines of the great British heretic Pelagius. Pelagius himself belonged to the narrow stratum of Celtic Britons, in what is now southern England, who served the Roman conquerors, and hence became Christian when the Empire was converted under Constantine. But, even after he had travelled to Rome and North Africa, his teaching retained a distinctly Celtic flavour. He was repelled by the lavish comforts of the Roman bishops and priests, and by the huge inequalities of wealth in Roman society, which were to him an affront to the simple morality of the gospel. And he hated too the fashionable doctrine of original sin, which taught that all men are helpless sinners, and can only be saved by the unmerited grace of God. Instead he believed that Jesus challenges each person to choose between good and evil; and that the good man should live simply, sharing his wealth with the poor. Moreover he urged people to regard Jesus, not as some remote divine figure, but as an intimate friend and brother. Pelagius was condemned as a heretic by the Roman hierarchy; but his robust morality, his assertion of individual freedom, and his devotion to the person of Jesus became for his Celtic compatriots the essence of the Christian faith.

◆   ◆   ◆

◆

The earliest evidence of Christianity in the British Isles is from southern England. A Roman villa at Chedworth near Gloucester, built around 180 A.D., has been uncovered by archaeologists, revealing various Christian monograms. And in the well of a villa at Appleshaw in Hampshire a pewter dish of similar date has been found, inscribed with the Chi-Rho symbol. The North African theologian Tertullian, writing in the year 200, mentions "places in Britain which have yielded to Christ"; and there are early accounts of the martyrdom of St. Alban during the persecution later that century. At the Council of Arles, held in 314, the list of participants mentions three British bishops, from London, Lincoln and York, indicating that Christianity had spread to all the major cities under Roman occupation.

But Christianity never took root in Roman Britain. The great majority of Christians were either Roman colonists, or Britons that had adopted Roman attitudes and customs, while to the Celtic tribesmen Christianity was despised as the religion of oppression, no better than the older Roman cults in which the emperor was held up for worship. Thus when the Roman Empire fell early in the fifth century, and Angles and Saxons swept across the south and east of the country, Christianity virtually disappeared. Only a handful of British Christians escaped into the hills of Wales, where they practised their religion in secret.

Yet by the early decades of the fifth century a new Christian mission was enjoying astonishing success, penetrating those areas of Celtic Britain which had never fallen to Roman conquest. This time it was not grand governors riding in elegant chariots who carried the gospel, but barefoot monks plodding the muddy lanes.

The first great saint of the Celtic church was Ninian, who remains unjustly obscure. He grew up a few miles north of Hadrian's Wall, late in the fourth century, and he travelled in Gaul where he encountered Martin of Tours.

Martin had founded the first western monastery in imitation of the desert fathers; and Ninian returned to his native land to set up his own monastery at Whithorn, a peninsula on the south-west coast of Scotland. Unlike Martin's community, which was admired but not imitated, Ninian's monastery became the model for countless similar groupings of monks and nuns throughout the Celtic lands. And Ninian is credited with converting many of the tribesmen in his area, establishing parish churches and training clergy.

The foundation of the Welsh church was similar to that of Scotland, its inspiration also being Martin's monastery at Tours. As the Roman legions retreated southwards through Gaul early in the fifth century to defend their motherland, many Cornish Christians set sail in tiny boats, heading for Wales to avoid the Anglo-Saxon raiders in eastern Britain. Monks from Tours established the first Welsh monastery in Llanbelig in Snowdonia; and soon afterwards Iltut, the most distinguished of these immigrants from Gaul, founded a community on the south coast of Wales. There he trained young men as evangelists, counting amongst his pupils David, who converted western Wales, and Samson, who sailed back across the seas to preach the gospel amongst the Celts of Brittany.

The most famous Celtic Christian is Patrick, who single-handedly converted the people of Ireland: between his arrival in about 435, and his death three decades later, the Christian gospel conquered the entire country. Yet he is an ambivalent figure, who in his later years was bitterly opposed by those he had converted. Like Ninian he trained in Gaul where he studied theology; but unlike Ninian he was deeply influenced by Roman attitudes and ideas. So in Ireland he tried to organise the church on Roman lines, with powerful bishops in grand cathedrals, enforcing strict moral and spiritual discipline. The Celts, however, while embracing the gospel he preached, spurned his ecclesiastical ambitions, preferring priests in mud chapels, and hermits in caves, who taught the faith by humble example. Under Patrick's successors, like Brigid and Kevin, the Celtic ways prevailed.

The Irish church was the jewel of Celtic Christianity, producing its finest poets, its most heroic saints, and its bravest evangelists. Not content with converting their own people, Irish monks built coracles in which they launched into the oceans, letting the wind carry them to new lands. Piran, along with numerous others, sailed southwards to Cornwall, which within a few decades had become dotted with monasteries and churches. Brendan went westwards, visiting the Faroe Islands, Iceland, and probably the east coast of America. And the fiery Columba, after a bitter dispute with the Irish church, sailed eastwards to the island of Iona, off the Scottish coast. From there Columba himself travelled throughout Scotland, converting tribal chiefs and kings, and establishing churches. And after his death missionaries from Iona, led by the gentle Aidan, took the gospel back into northern and central England, winning the allegiance of many Anglo-Saxon rulers.

◆ ◆ ◆

◆

The heart of the Celtic fire was the monastery. The Celtic monastery was usually started by a hermit, who cleared a piece of forest and built himself a hut. Gradually others would come to join him, clearing some more woodland and erecting huts nearby. Then in their midst they would build a chapel, a simple wooden frame covered in turfs. Sometimes these communities grew to no more than ten or twenty people, but often they consisted of hundreds or even thousands of men and women, forming by far the largest settlements in the whole of the British Isles. And they were constantly spawning new communities, as individual monks and nuns, weary of the bustle of the large monastery, went off into the forest to live as hermits; and soon others would come, to form another monastery.

In continental Europe the simplicity of Martin's community at Tours was being replaced by a more elaborate form of monasticism instituted by Benedict, in which every aspect of the monks' life was governed by a strict Rule, and the abbot had absolute authority. In Britain and Ireland, by contrast, the monks and nuns enjoyed a high degree of freedom, and their way of life remained simple and flexible. They each worked out their own pattern of prayer and meditation, meeting only once a day for worship. With a few exceptions they neither ploughed the land nor kept livestock, preferring instead to go out alone or in groups into the forest to collect berries, nuts and roots to eat. The abbot was seen not as a ruler to whom obedience was owed, but rather as a wise spiritual guide from whom to seek advice; and many of the larger communities had a number of abbots, with the individual monk choosing whom he preferred as spiritual adviser. Every monastery had huts available for travellers and for the sick, and the monks were expected to share with them some of the food they had gathered.

The Druid priestly communities had run schools which were renowned for their erudition, drawing young men and women from as far away as Gaul and Spain. The Celtic monasteries continued this tradition, and their schools became a vital tool of evangelism. It soon became the custom even for heathen tribesmen, especially the chiefs and landowners, to send their children to a monastic school; the child would return imbued with the new religion, and thence, when he grew to adulthood, spread it amongst his own clan. The pupils were expected to share fully in the rigours of monastic life, living in grass huts and gathering food from the forest, but they were also taught to read, write and, above all, sing; and undoubtedly the monasteries stimulated the great flowering of Celtic literature and poetry.

Some of the monasteries also began to train young men as evangelists, to go out on foot to the remotest farmsteads to preach the gospel. Three of these evangelistic monasteries remain even today places of pilgrimage: Armagh in Northern Ireland, founded by Patrick himself; Columba's Iona; and, in imitation of

Iona, Lindisfarne off the northern coast, founded by Aidan. Armagh rapidly became the centre of the Irish church, training men to form new monasteries throughout the country. Columba tried to set up a similar network of monasteries around Ireland, which provoked furious opposition. But his dream was fulfilled in Scotland where, after his exile to Iona, he sent out evangelists to convert the Picts: to a quite remarkable extent the monasteries he established came to exercise not only spiritual but also political power, forging bonds of peace between the warring tribes. Thus Columba succeeded where the Roman legions for four centuries had failed.

Having conquered Scotland for Christ, the monks turned their sights southwards to England; and, after one abortive mission, sent Aidan, whose gentle humour won the hearts of both the kings and peasants of northern England. He attracted young men of the highest calibre to Lindisfarne, and he personally trained them in the arts of preaching and teaching. Equal in importance to all these famous places was Iltut's community on the south coast of Wales, whose site is now covered with a car park and café. Iltut was the most erudite theologian of the Celtic church who, in his spare moments, turned his mind to inventing new agricultural implements to aid the local peasants. He taught his young priests to be efficient managers, as well as effective speakers: thus David in western Wales and Samson in Brittany created a pattern of church organisation which was the envy of many Roman bishops.

The most extraordinary feature of the Celtic mission was the "pilgrims." Men like Columba and David had clear plans to convert specific territories; but numerous others set out quite aimlessly, trusting that God would lead them. They were content if they encountered no one, and to live as hermits; but equally, if they met people on the road or in the villages, they would speak of Christ. Some just walked, remaining within their native land; but others set out in tiny boats, often without either sails or oars to guide them. The

* * *

•

most famous of these seafarers was Brendan, but even he found both hermits and entire communities of monks on the remote islands he visited, who had themselves set out from Ireland and Britain previously. The *Anglo-Saxon Chronicle* contains a delightful description of three such pilgrims arriving on a beach in southern England where King Alfred was encamped: when they discovered that the king was already a Christian, they asked for fresh supplies of food, and continued their journey. Many Celtic monks reached the northern coast of Europe, preaching to the Angles, Saxons and Viking tribes who were themselves invading Britain.

◆ ◆ ◆

The year 597 saw both the death of Columba in Iona, and the arrival of Augustine, sent by the pope, in Canterbury. The Celtic church had steadfastly rejected the authority of Rome, asserting that each individual is answerable directly to God for his actions. To successive popes this attitude smacked of the

85897 • • 274 Brescia College Library
          17 103 Owensboro, Kentucky
              • C 394

Pelagian heresy; and for over a century, in the name of doctrinal orthodoxy, Rome had tried in vain to bring the stubborn Celts under its rule. When Ethelbert, the Saxon king of Kent, who was himself a heathen, married a Christian wife sympathetic to Rome, Pope Gregory seized the opportunity for a fresh mission. Without consulting the Celtic church, he appointed Augustine bishop of the entire British Isles, with the task of "instructing the unlearned, encouraging the weak, and correcting the obstinate." Augustine arrived with forty monks at Thanet; and, having won the support of Ethelbert, he sought contact with the Celts, to persuade them to accept his authority.

Augustine had two meetings with the Celtic leaders. The first, on the banks of the Severn estuary, was inconclusive. Augustine argued that if the Celtic church accepted his authority, their common mission to the heathen of Britain would be far more effective than the Celts working alone. It was a clever point, designed to appeal to the evangelistic Celts;

* * *

Brescia College Library
Owensboro, Kentucky

but they also knew that Roman rule would impose new styles of worship, and a different method of calculating the date of Easter. So they asked for time to reflect and pray before giving their answer, arranging another meeting with Augustine some time later. The Celtic leaders held various fasts and councils, to seek God's will; and they went to see an old hermit—whose name goes unrecorded—whom they considered the wisest man in Britain. The hermit advised that they should only accept Augustine as their bishop if he showed himself meek and lowly at their next meeting, by rising from his chair to greet them. The second meeting with Augustine was a disaster. Not only did he fail to rise, but his attitude had turned hostile: he accused the Celts of heresy, defying God's will by remaining divided from the universal church; hence they must pledge allegiance to the pope, or face eternal damnation. The Celts remained impassive during Augustine's diatribe; then at the end they announced that, since he had not risen to greet them, he would surely hold them of no account if they acknowledged him as bishop.

For the next half century Celt and Catholic were locked in bitter competition. Pope Gregory had an elaborate plan to divide England into two provinces, based on the chief Roman towns of London and York, each of which would have an archbishop; these would be subdivided into twelve dioceses, each with its own bishop. Augustine and his successors immediately sought to enact this scheme. In London they met furious heathen opposition, and so were forced back into Kent, where the archbishop installed himself at Canterbury. Further north Celtic and Catholic priests vied to win the allegiance of various kings and chiefs. At first the Catholics gained the upper hand, with an archbishop being welcomed at York; but then the Celtic mission from Iona, led by Aidan and Cuthbert, won the hearts of kings and peasants alike, forcing the Catholic archbishop to flee for his life.

Finally, however, it was the Celts themselves who undermined their own cause, through their generosity of spirit. While the Catholics despised all things Celtic, the Celts were happy to learn from Catholic theology and practise, even sending young men to Europe to study under the great Catholic teachers. Thus an increasing number of Celts yearned for a fusion of the two traditions, looking forward to a united church of Britain. In 664 a synod was called at the great Celtic monastery of Whitby to seek such unity. Hilda, the formidable abbess, had long encouraged her monks and nuns to read both Catholic and Celtic literature, and was eager to find a compromise between the two sides. But the outcome was an almost total defeat for the Celts.

The leader of the Catholics was Wilfred. A native of Northumbria, he had entered the monastery at Lindisfarne at the age of fourteen; but after a spell studying theology in Gaul and Rome, he had become a militant supporter of the Catholic cause, eager to sweep away all traces of Celtic ways. The

* * *

*

Celts were led by a stubborn, hot-headed monk, Colman, who, unlike many of his forebears, was unwilling to bend on even the smallest issue. When Colman had finished his opening address to the synod, Wilfred accused the Celts of narrow-minded bigotry: "The only people stupid enough to disagree with the whole world are these Scots, and their obstinate adherents the Picts and Britons, who inhabit only a tiny portion of these two islands in the ocean." Later, to Colman's disgust, Wilfred invoked the name of Columba and his pious successors at Iona, saying that if they were alive, they would immediately submit to Catholic authority. "Although your fathers were holy men," Wilfred added, "do not imagine that they, a small number in the far corner of this remote island, are to be preferred to the universal Church throughout the world." Once Oswy, the powerful Celtic king of Northumbria, was won over by Wilfred's arguments, the Celtic cause was lost. And Colman with his companions stormed out of the synod, retreating to an island off

◆　◆　◆

◆

the west coast of Ireland, where in majestic isolation they upheld the Celtic ways.

❖ ❖ ❖

Today in the various denominations of Britain and Ireland there is a single visible reminder of the Celtic past. Throughout the rest of Europe church buildings generally have a rounded wall behind the altar, in the style of the ancient Roman basilica; in British churches, by contrast, the east ends are square, in the Celtic style.

But, although the outward signs are few, the Celtic fire has continued to burn. The great German theologian Karl Barth a few years ago described British Christianity as "incurably Pelagian." The rugged individualism of the Celtic monk, his conviction that each person is free to choose between good and evil, and his insistence that faith must be practical as well as spiritual remain hallmarks of Christians in Britain. And the British imagination has remained rooted in nature, witnessed by the pastoral poetry and landscape painting in which Britain excels; indeed that peculiar British obsession with gardening is Celtic in origin. Visitors to the British Isles are often shocked at how few people attend church each Sunday. Yet to the Britons, church-goers as well as absentees, the primary test of faith is not religious observance, but daily behaviour towards our neighbours—and towards one's pets, livestock and plants!

For over a millennium the treasures of Celtic poetry, and the wisdom of the great Celtic saints, lay largely hidden. Manuscripts were buried in monastic libraries or private collections, written in the ancient languages that few could understand. Last century, however, scholars began to unearth these old writings, translating them into modern English; and travellers visited remote islands and villages in Ireland and Scotland, writing down the poems, prayers and stories that had been passed orally from one generation to another. A few of these translations and transcriptions enjoy wide popularity, such as Eleanor Hull's "Be Thou My Vision" (now a favourite hymn, set to a traditional Irish melody), the various versions of St. Patrick's Breastplate, and Dr. Alexander Carmichael's collection of old Hebridean verses.

The present book is culled from the widest possible sources and scholarly works (see the bibliography, pp. 246–48). And as a frequent childhood visitor to Ireland, where a branch of my family owned vast tracts of remote and beautiful countryside, I heard from the mouths of old family retainers some of the ancient stories and poems. In compiling this collection, I have put different sources and translations side by side, and made a new version, using modern forms of speech. For the purposes of scholarship this may seem to lack precision; but, since the primary sources are mainly oral, the editor's task must be to convey the spirit of the original piece, rather than pursue literal accuracy.

The Celts were tireless pilgrims. No sooner had a saint died than his hermitage or monastery became the focus of ardent devotion. So, for those who want to follow in their ancient footsteps, I have added at the end of this book a plan for a modern Celtic pilgrimage. There are numerous sites around the British Isles containing Celtic crosses, and even beehive huts once used by Celtic monks. And even where no artefacts remain, the great centres of the Celtic church, such as Iona, Lindisfarne, Whithorn, Kildare and St. Davids, most powerfully evoke its spirit. I personally have enjoyed wonderful holidays visiting Celtic sites, so I offer a brief guide for other pilgrims.

Like most modern inhabitants of Britain, I can make little claim to Celtic ancestry: even my Irish forebears were of continental origin, acquiring their lands in the seventeenth century. But all of us born and bred in the British Isles, whatever blood runs in our veins, have the Celtic fire in our hearts. To read the stories and meditations of the ancient Celts is to add fuel to that fire; and it is for that purpose I offer this book.

THE CONFESSION
OF PATRICK

Patrick's confession is one of the few pieces of Celtic writing—and certainly the earliest—where authorship is known. And it is unusual also in being autobiographical: Patrick is defending himself against a charge of misusing funds he has been given, and so tells the story of his life to show the sincerity of his purpose. In the process he reveals his evangelistic method. He would win over a local chief, and then persuade the chief to let one of his sons join his mission. He would also beg for gifts from the chief, which could be used to win the friendship of other chiefs. It was his huge success, combined with the large number of valuable objects that passed through his hands, which evoked the jealousy of other evangelists, prompting them to accuse him of corruption. Patrick also recounts his

travels to remote regions, where he preached to the
ordinary peasants and ordained priests to serve them.

◆ A SLAVE IN IRELAND ◆

I, Patrick, a sinner, and the most unlearned
and the lowest of all the faithful, utterly despised by many. My father was Calpornius, a
deacon, and my grandfather Potitus, a priest.
I was brought up near the town of Bannaven
Tiburnia. At the age of sixteen, before I knew
God, I was taken captive and shipped to Ireland, along with thousands of others.

When I arrived in Ireland I was sent to tend
sheep. I used to pray many times each day;
and, as I prayed, I felt God's love fill my heart
and strengthen my faith. Soon I was saying
up to a hundred prayers each day, and almost
as many at night. I had to stay all night in
the forests and on the mountains, looking after
the sheep, and I would wake to pray before
dawn in all weathers, snow, frost and rain; I
felt no fear, nor did I feel sleepy, because the
Spirit was so fervent within me.

It was there one night, while I was asleep,

that I heard a voice speaking to me: "You do well to fast and pray, for soon you shall be returning to your home country." And shortly afterwards I heard another voice: "See, your ship is ready." The ship was not near, but was two hundred miles away in a place where I knew nobody and had never visited. I immediately fled from the man who had enslaved me for six years, and in the strength of God travelled to the coast. During the whole journey I met no dangers whatever.

On the day that I arrived the ship was ready to set sail, and I insisted that I come aboard. But the captain became angry, saying, "You are wasting your time asking to come with us." When I heard this I left the ship to go back to the hut where I was staying, and began to pray. But before I had finished my prayer, I heard one of the crew shouting loudly after me: "Come quickly!" When I got back to the ship they said to me, "Come aboard—we'll take you on trust, treating you as a friend." I refused to be too intimate with them, for fear of God; but I was happy to befriend them, in the hope of bringing them to faith in Jesus Christ. We set sail at once.

After three days at sea, we reached land. For the next month we travelled on foot through a vast region where no one lived; eventually our food ran out, and we became extremely hungry. One of my companions said: "Tell us, Christian, you say that your God is great and all-powerful, so why can you not pray for us, and save us from starving?" I replied, "Turn with all your heart to the Lord my God, to whom nothing is impossible, and today he will provide abundant food." And that is precisely what happened: a herd of pigs appeared before us, and we killed enough of them to satisfy our hunger. After this my companions gave thanks to God, and I gained respect in their eyes.

◆ THE CALL OF IRELAND ◆

At last I reached my home, and spent the next few years with my family. They begged that now, after suffering so many hardships, I should never leave them again. But one night in a dream I saw a man coming from Ireland, whose name was Victoricus, carrying countless letters. He gave one of them to me, and I read the heading: "The Voice of the Irish." And as I looked at these words, I heard a voice coming from the Forest of Foclut in the far west of Ireland, calling me: "We implore you, young man, to return and walk among us." My heart seemed to be breaking and I could read no more.

During another night I heard a voice—I do not know whether it was within me or beside me, God only knows—whose words I could not understand, except the final sentence: "He who lay down his life for you, it is he that speaks within you." And I awoke full of joy. And sometime later I saw him praying within me: I was, as it were, inside my own body and I could hear his voice. He was praying most powerfully. I was dumbfounded, wondering who it could be praying within me; but at the end of the prayer he said that he was the Spirit. And then I awoke, remembering the apostle's words: "The Spirit helps us in our weakness; for we do not know how to pray as we ought, but the Spirit himself intercedes for us with sighs too deep for words."

Finally I knew I must go to Ireland. But I did not give way to the Spirit's promptings until I was utterly exhausted. The Lord thus broke down my stubbornness, and moulded me according to his will, making me fit to do work which once had been far beyond me. I could now dedicate myself to the salvation of others, whereas once I had been indifferent even to my own salvation.

• MISSIONARY LABOURS •

It would be tedious to relate all my labours in detail, or even in part; what matters is that God often forgave my stupidity and careless-ness, and took pity upon me thousands and thousands of times. There were many who tried to prevent my mission, saying behind my back: "What is this fellow up to, talking to God's enemies?" They were not being ma-licious, but were unhappy that a man so un-educated as I am should conduct such a mission. But, though I am untalented, I have done my best always to be honest and sincere, with Christians and heathen alike.

I have baptised many thousands of people, but never asked as much as a halfpenny in return. Despite being such an unexceptional person myself, I have trained and ordained priests throughout the country; but I have never asked even the price of a shoe as reward. Instead, I have spent whatever money I possessed for the benefit of the common people.

I have travelled in the remotest regions of the country, where no Christian has ever been before, and there I have baptised and confirmed people, and ordained priests; and I have done so with a joyful heart and tireless spirit. I have given presents to kings and persuaded them to release slaves; and I have inspired the sons of kings to travel with me on my missions. I and my companions have at times been arrested and put in irons, and our captors have been eager to kill us; yet the Lord has always set us free.

But I now see that in this present world I

am exalted above my true merit, and I am more privileged than I deserve. I am more suited to poverty and adversity than to riches and luxury—for the Lord Christ was poor for our sakes. Yet in truth I have no wealth of my own, and every day I expect to be killed, betrayed or reduced to slavery. I am frightened of none of these things, because my heart is set on the riches of heaven.

I now commend my soul to God, for whom, despite my obscurity, I have served as ambassador—indeed, in choosing me for this noble task, he has shown that he is no respecter of persons, because I am the least of his servants. May God never separate me from his people on this island, which stands at the very edge of the earth. And may God always make me a faithful witness to him, until he calls me to heaven.

◆ PATRICK'S CREED ◆

There is no other God except God the Father; nor was there ever in times past, nor will there ever be in the future. He is the beginning of all things, and himself has no beginning. He possesses all things, but is possessed by none.

His Son Jesus Christ has been with the Father before the beginning; and through him all things were created, both spiritual and material. He became man, and conquered death; and was taken back into heaven to the Father.

The Father has given to his Son power over all things in heaven and on earth, and under the earth, that every tongue should confess that Jesus Christ is Lord.

He has poured upon us his Spirit, so that our spirits are overflowing. Through his Spirit we receive the promise of eternal life. And in his Spirit we are taught to trust and obey the Father, and, with Christ, become his sons and daughters.

BRIGID'S CITY

Brigid was the name both of the Druid goddess of fertility and the great abbess of Kildare; and in Irish devotion the old Druid cult became, almost unchanged, the cult of the Christian saint—even enjoying the same feast-day, 1 February. As a result the historical Brigid is largely lost under a welter of legend. Happily, however, the stories of her childhood, showing her as a stubborn headstrong girl, have the ring of truth; and one of these stories, in which her father tried and failed to sell her as a slave, is one of the gems of Celtic literature. The monastery which she founded under a huge oak tree (hence the name Kildare, which means Cell of the Oak) became the largest settlement in the whole of Ireland. She ruled it like a queen, and she

*was renowned for her generous hospitality to the poor
and sick. Kildare became known as the "City of the
Poor," and it is Brigid's regal hospitality which is
celebrated in the songs about her.*

◆ THE HEADSTRONG CHILD ◆

Brigid's father was extremely wealthy, own-
ing much land and many precious objects,
and his larder was filled with fine food. But
Brigid would raid the larder, and give the
food to the poor and needy in the neighbourhood. This greatly angered her father,
who decided to try and sell her. So one day
he grabbed his daughter, and threw her into
the back of his chariot, crying: "It is not out
of kindness or honour that I am taking you
in the chariot; but I am going to sell you to
the King of Leinster as a slave, to grind his
corn."

When they arrived at the king's fortress,
Brigid's father unbuckled his sword, leaving it
in the chariot beside Brigid, so that he could
go to the king unarmed, as a sign of respect.

But, as soon as her father had left the chariot, a leper appeared, begging Brigid to help him; so she picked up the sword and gave it to him.

Meanwhile in the fortress her father was asking the king to buy her. "Why do you want to sell your daughter?" the king asked. "That's easy to answer," he replied; "she is giving away all my wealth to poor, worthless men." "Well," said the king, "bring her in, and show her to me." So they both went out to the chariot. Her father noticed at once the sword was missing, and asked Brigid what had happened to it. "I gave it to a leper who came begging," she replied. Her father flew into a wild rage and began to beat his daughter.

"Stop," cried the king, and beckoned Brigid over to him. "Why do you steal your father's property and give it away?" the king asked. "If I had the power," answered Brigid, "I would steal all your royal wealth, and give it to Christ's brothers and sisters." The king turned to Brigid's father: "I am afraid your daughter is too good for me; I could never win her obedience."

And so Brigid, by her own kindness, was saved from slavery.

◆BRIGID'S FEAST◆

I should like a great lake of finest ale
For the King of kings.
I should like a table of the choicest food
For the family of heaven.
Let the ale be made from the fruits of
    faith,
And the food be forgiving love.

I should welcome the poor to my feast,
For they are God's children.
I should welcome the sick to my feast,
For they are God's joy.
Let the poor sit with Jesus at the highest
    place,
And the sick dance with the angels.

God bless the poor,
God bless the sick,
And bless our human race.

◆　◆　◆

◆

God bless our food,
God bless our drink,
All homes, O God, embrace.

◆ A HYMN TO ST. BRIGID ◆

Her heart contained no poison, no snake lurked within her breast; she nursed no grudges, harboured no resentments.

In the spiritual field where she sowed, the weather was always right.

When she sowed the seeds of the gospel in people's hearts, the soft rain would fall, so the seeds would sprout.

When she taught Christians how to grow in the image of Christ, the sun shone in the day, and the rain fell at night, so the fruits of good works would swell.

When she welcomed the sick and the dying, the weather was warm and dry, to prepare their souls for God's harvest.

Now in heaven she intercedes for us, sending upon us the gentle dew of God's grace.

◆　◆　◆

◆

Sit safely, Brigid, on your throne. From the banks of the Liffey to the coast you are the princess of our children, ruling with the angels over us.

God's intentions for Ireland are far beyond men's reach. Though the Liffey be yours to-day, once it belonged to others.

Loegaire was king to the sea, then Allen, and Crimthenn the Brave. Under Ireland's plains they lie buried; no empire has endured.

Swords tangled on the battlefield, then a sudden shout of triumph. Horns shrieking over a thousand heads; another great victory won.

The clang of hammers on anvil, fashioning swords for war. The songs from the tongues of bards, singing the glories of kings.

The clanking of chains on soldiers' wrists, the flashing blades of five-edged spears, fine horses riding into battle, fine ladies watching from afar.

◆ ◆ ◆

◆

The wide open plains, and the high purple mountains are the scenes of ancient triumphs; but no empire has endured.

We reject the spells of witches, we spurn the worship of Druids. The forts of pagan kings lie empty and overgrown.

It is Brigid's smile that shines across rivers and grassy plains. It is Brigid's frown that withers the pride of pagan kings.

Brigid, in the land which I love your fame is greatest of all. While the power of kings is fragile, your empire shall always endure.

Your rule is the rule of God, built on eternal rock. This fertile land is your church, its highest peak your throne.

THE VOYAGE OF BRENDAN

The story of Brendan's voyage across the Atlantic in a tiny coracle is the most popular tale in all Celtic literature: in the centuries after his death the Latin version of the story circulated throughout Europe, and was in turn translated into French, Flemish and Saxon. Brendan was abbot of Clonfert, a large monastery in central Ireland. One Lent he went back to the southwestern tip of the country, where he had grown up, and spent the season on top of a high mountain overlooking the ocean, fasting and praying. Other pilgrims had set sail before, in search of the "Island of Promise," and Brendan decided to follow their example. He recruited fourteen other monks to join him, and they built a coracle out of oxhides tanned with oak bark. We can only infer their route from the descriptions of the *places they visited; and these suggest they made a giant loop via the Faroe Islands and Iceland to Newfoundland, returning via the Azores, which they took to be the Island of Promise.*

◆BRENDAN SETS SAIL◆

Brendan chose fourteen monks from his community, took them to the chapel, and made this proposal to them. "My beloved fellow soldiers in the spiritual war: I beg your help, because my heart is set upon a single desire. If it be God's will, I want to seek out the Island of Promise of which our forefathers have spoken. Will you come with me? What are your feelings?" As soon as he had finished speaking, the monks replied with one voice. "Father, your desire is ours also. Have we not forsaken our parents and abandoned our property in order to put ourselves totally into your hands? We are ready to go with you, for better for worse, so long as it is God's will."

During the next forty days Brendan and his companions took food only every third day, to prepare themselves physically and spiritually for their journey. Then they bade farewell to their community, and set off to the coast. There, in a narrow cove, they made a coracle, using iron tools. The ribs and frame were carved out of wood, and then covered with oxhide, tanned in oak bark. They smeared the seams with grease to make them waterproof, storing extra hides and grease in the coracle for repairs. Then a mast was erected, with a simple sail attached, and food for forty days was loaded into the vessel. When all was ready Brendan ordered his monks aboard, the sail was hoisted, and the coracle was swept out to sea.

For the next two weeks the wind was fair, so that they did no more than steady the sail. But then the wind fell, and they had to row, day after day. When their strength eventually failed, Brendan comforted them: "Have no fear, brothers, for God is our captain and our pilot; so take in the oars, and set the sail, letting him blow us where he wills." So they stopped rowing and again hoisted the sail. From time to time the wind blew, but they had no idea in what direction they were sailing.

At last they sighted an island on the horizon. A fair wind sprang up which carried them to its shore, and Brendan ordered them to disembark. Walking round the island they saw great streams of water gushing down from the hills, teaming with all kinds of fish. And there were numerous flocks of sheep, all pure white and so enormous that they seemed to blot out the ground from view.

The day of their arrival was Good Friday, and Brendan ordered the brethren to take one of the sheep to symbolise the Lamb of God. So they chose the finest animal, and one of the monks tied a cord around its horn so he could lead it like a pet. Then suddenly a man appeared, carrying a basket of bread baked in hot ashes and other food, which he laid at Brendan's feet. With tears in his eyes, he cried: "O precious pearl of God, what have I done

◆ ◆ ◆

46

◆

to deserve this honour, of providing food and drink for you with my own hands in this holy season?" "My son," Brendan replied, "our Lord Jesus Christ has decided that this is the place where we shall remember his redeeming death." "Yes," said the man, "but Christ also wills that you celebrate his resurrection on the island you can see close by."

Then the man asked the monks to sit down, and he began serving them with food. Later, after they had eaten, he went away to collect food for them to take to the other island, and he carried it down to the coracle. He said to Brendan, "Your boat can hold no more, but in eight days time I will come over with sufficient food to last until Pentecost." The following morning Brendan and his companions climbed back into their coracle to row over to the other island. But before setting off Brendan asked the man why the sheep on the island grew so large. "There is nobody on the island to milk them," he replied; "and since the winter here is never cold, they can stay on the grass and feed all the year round." Then Brendan and the man blessed one another, and the man pushed the coracle out to sea.

When they arrived on the other island they rowed into the mouth of a stream on the southern shore; the monks then climbed out, pulling the coracle upstream against the current for about a mile. Finally they reached a spring which was the stream's source, and Brendan declared that this was the place to celebrate Easter. "Even if we had brought no food," he declared, "the stream would have provided all the nourishment we need." Beyond the spring on the shallow hills stood a tall tree, with pure white birds perching on every branch. One of the birds flew down to welcome Brendan, landing on his shoulder and flapping its wings with joy. Then at dusk, when the monks began to sing their evening prayers, the birds joined in, chirping in perfect harmony, and beating their wings to the rhythm of the monks' chants.

The next morning the monks began their Easter worship, continuing for eight days. At the end the man came from the other island with more food, and the monks remained amongst the birds until Pentecost. The birds attended every service, singing like the finest choir. Finally after Pentecost Brendan ordered the monks to fill their flasks with water from the spring, and the man from the other island loaded the coracle with food for forty days; and once again they set out into the open sea.

• ICEBERGS •

Brendan and his monks spent three months sailing across the vast ocean, with only the sea and the sky for company, not knowing in what direction they were moving. They ate only every third day.

One day they saw a column rising up from the sea. It seemed quite close, but in fact it took them three days to reach it. When they drew near, Brendan looked upwards, and could hardly see the summit because it was so high—it seemed to pierce the sky. The column shone like silver, and yet was clear like glass, and was as hard as marble—indeed, the monks could not decide from what material it was made.

Brendan ordered the monks to take in their oars, and lower the sail. He then directed the monks to grab hold of the column, and draw the coracle into an opening at the base. "Let us inspect this wonderful creation of God," he said. Once in the opening the sea was perfectly clear; and looking beneath them they could see that the column went down into the water as deeply as it rose to the sky. And the sun shone through the column to create a dazzling white light.

They spent a whole day sailing round the column. Even when the sun was behind the column, they could still feel its heat shining through. Then they sailed onwards.

◆ ICELAND ◆

Eight days later they caught sight of a bare, rocky island, without grass or trees, covered with slag. "Brothers," said Brendan, "I feel most fearful of this island. I have no wish to land on it, or even to go near; yet the wind is carrying us towards it." As they got closer they heard noise like the blowing of bellows, followed by the din of a hammer on an anvil. Brendan made the sign of the cross, praying, "O Lord Jesus Christ, deliver us from this evil island."

But hardly had he finished praying when one of the inhabitants appeared, his body grimy with the fire and smoke. He caught sight of the coracle, and turned back. Brendan again made the sign of the cross, crying, "Let us flee from this place—hoist the sail and row as fast as you can." But before they could move the man appeared again, carrying a huge piece of blazing slag in a pair of tongs: he hurled it at the coracle, and it hit the water just beyond them, sending up a thick cloud of steam.

As the coracle sailed away, all the inhabitants of the island rushed down to the beach, each carrying a glowing lump of slag, which they flung at Brendan and his companions. Soon the sea all round the coracle was hissing like a boiling cauldron. "Soldiers of Christ," Brendan called to his brethren, "put on your

spiritual armour and stand firm in the faith;
for we are at the gates of hell itself." Then as
the smoke subsided they could see a high
mountain to the north; and it began to belch
white smoke from its peak, throwing burning
slag down its slopes.

At last the wind turned southwards, carrying the coracle swiftly away from the burning island. As they looked back they could
see the mountain vomiting flames, then sucking
the flames back into itself, until the whole island, right down to the water's edge, glowed
like a pyre.

◆ NEWFOUNDLAND ◆

After many days Brendan and his fellow warriors in Christ saw land in the distance, and
this inspired them to row faster. "Do not ex-
haust your strength," Brendan urged them;
"God will bring us to land in his own good
time."

When they reached the shore the cliffs
were so steep that they could see no place to
land. So they sailed round until they found a

small creek, just wide enough for the prow of the coracle. Brendan got out first, and climbed up the cliff. At the top he found two caves facing one another. From the mouth of one cave a tiny spring gushed forth, and inside the other cave was a hermit. The hermit came out to greet Brendan, embracing him; and then the hermit asked Brendan to invite the other monks up to join them. As the monks reached the top of the cliff, the hermit kissed each one, and called them by name. The monks were astonished at this prophetic gift of knowing their names, and also were amazed at the hermit's appearance: he had no clothes, but was covered from head to toe with thick, white hair.

The hermit introduced himself as Paul. Brendan asked how he came to this remote place, and how long he had lived there. Paul replied: "For forty years I belonged to St. Patrick's monastery in Ireland, where I was in charge of the cemetery. One day Patrick himself appeared to me in a vision, ordering me to go down to the shore where a small boat would be waiting for me. The next morning I walked to the beach, and there indeed was a boat. I got in, and the wind carried me straight here. Once I had arrived I knew that this was where God wanted me to live. So I pushed the boat away with my feet, and at that moment the wind changed direction, carrying the boat swiftly back towards Ireland. Then a seal emerged from the waves, with a fish in its mouth for my dinner; and on every third day ever since then a seal has always appeared, and laid a fish at my feet. I have now been here thirty years."

Brendan and his companions praised God for his mercy, and asked if they might stay with him for a time. "Sadly you cannot stay here," Paul replied; "God wants you to continue this very day onwards towards the Island of Promise." Paul then loaded the coracle with extra fish that the seals had brought the previous day, and Brendan and his companions embarked, with heavy hearts. Paul blessed them and pushed their coracle out into the waves; and a strong wind carried them south-wards.

For forty days the coracle was blown hither and thither across the ocean, and the monks' only source of nourishment was the fish which Paul had given them. Then on the evening of the fortieth day a dark fog descended over the coracle, so the monks could barely see one another. An hour later the fog disappeared and to their astonishment they discovered that they had landed on a beach. The sun shone brilliantly, and in front of them lay a vast orchard, its trees laden with huge fruit. The monks ran up the beach to the trees, and ate their fill. Then they began walking inland, and for four days travelled through green, fertile country, filled with fruit trees and watered by springs of clear, sweet water gushing up from the ground.

Eventually they reached a fast-flowing river, too wide and deep for them to cross. As they

were pondering what to do a young man appeared, embraced each monk in turn, and—
like Paul the hermit—called each by name.
"Welcome," he exclaimed, "you have at last
reached the land you have been seeking all
these years. The Lord Jesus did not allow you
to find it immediately, because first he wanted
to show you the wonders of the ocean. Now
fill your coracle to the brim with jewels, and
return to your native land. The day of your
own final journey is close, and soon you shall
be at peace with your forefathers. Then, after
many more years have passed, this island will
be revealed to your successors, when they
need to flee from persecution."

Brendan and his companions gathered fruit
and all kinds of precious stones, bade the
young man farewell, and returned to their coracle. They sailed out into the dark fog.

•BRENDAN'S RETURN•

The wind took the coracle directly back to
the beach in the south-west of Ireland from

which they had first set sail. Their community
was overjoyed at Brendan's return, praising
God for letting them see again their beloved
abbot. Brendan too was filled with love for his
brethren, and he recounted all the wonders
of the ocean which God had revealed. Finally
he told them of the prophecy of the young
man on the Island of Promise, that soon he
would set off on his final journey. So he put
his affairs in order, bade farewell to his brethren for the last time, lay down on his bed,
and crossed the great spiritual ocean to his
Maker.

◆ BRENDAN'S PRAYER ON THE MOUNTAIN ◆

Shall I abandon, O King of Mysteries, the soft
comforts of home? Shall I turn my back on
my native land, and my face towards the sea?

Shall I put myself wholly at the mercy of God,
without silver, without a horse, without fame
and honour? Shall I throw myself wholly on

◆   ◆   ◆

◆

the King of kings, without sword and shield, without food and drink, without a bed to lie on?

Shall I say farewell to my beautiful land, placing myself under Christ's yoke? Shall I pour out my heart to him, confessing my manifold sins and begging forgiveness, tears streaming down my cheeks?

Shall I leave the prints of my knees on the sandy beach, a record of my final prayer in my native land? Shall I then suffer every kind of wound that the sea can inflict?

Shall I take my tiny coracle across the wide, sparkling ocean? O King of the Glorious Heaven, shall I go of my own choice upon the sea?

O Christ, will you help me on the wild waves?

COLUMBA'S
ISLAND

Although others like Ninian and Mungo had already
preached the Christian gospel in Scotland, Columba
can justly be claimed as her apostle, penetrating the
northern and western regions. Until the age of about
forty Columba was busy setting up a network of
monasteries throughout Ireland, including those at
Derry and Kells, as centres of education and evangelism. He was a shrewd diplomat, securing the pat-
ronage of kings and chiefs by supporting them against
their enemies. But in 563 he found himself on the
losing side of one of the bloodiest battles in Irish history, and was forced to flee in a tiny coracle to
Scotland. On the island of Iona he established a monastery which was soon attracting large numbers from

the mainland. And he went on various missions, using his diplomatic skills to astonishing effect, even at one stage being asked to appoint a new king of southern Scotland. A series of laments, supposedly by Columba himself, relate the story of his exile, his homesickness for Ireland, and his enjoyment of Iona. The anecdote of Columba trying to live on nettle soup is typical of the affectionate stories that were told of this iron-willed man. The account of his death is both joyful and dramatic.

◆ COLUMBA'S JOURNEY ◆

Great is the speed of my coracle, its stern turned upon Derry. Great is the grief in my heart, my face set upon Alba.

My coracle sings on the waves, yet my eyes are filled with tears. I know God blows me east, yet my heart still pulls me west.

My eyes shall never again feast on the beauty of Eire's shore. My ears shall never again hear the cries of her tiny babes.

Though my body speeds to Alba, my mind is

fixed on Eire: upon Ulster, Munster and Meath, on her beauty from Lenny to Linn.

In Alba their hearts are hard, their tempers jealous and harsh; their bodies plagued with disease, their clothes thin and scanty.

But in Eire their hearts are soft, their tempers gentle and wise; their women fair and kind, their men stout and strong.

The orchards bend double with fruit, the bushes are blue with sloes; the plains are lush with grass, the cattle healthy and fat.

Tuneful are the songs of the monks, and tuneful the chants of the birds; courteous the words of young men, and wise the words of the old.

My heart is broken in two for love of my beautiful land. If death should suddenly take me, the cause is grief for my home.

If all Alba were mine, from its centre out to its coast, I would gladly exchange it for a field in a valley of Durrow or Derry.

◆ ◆ ◆

◆

Carry westwards my blessing, to Eire carry my love. Yet carry also my blessing east to the shores of Alba.

•COLUMBA IN EXILE•

It would be delightful, O Son of Mary, to plough the blue seas to Ireland, to measure the height of their waves.

We would sail around Moyn-Olurg, and plunge down through Lough Foyle, hearing the swans in sweet song.

Flocks of gulls would rejoice, screaming and screeching with joy, as our boat arrived in port.

In Ireland I was a man of power; when I left I was filled with grief. In exile my soul was heavy.

I was forced to cross the sea. If only I had never waged that wretched battle at Cul Drenne.

Oh happy my younger self, happy in my cell at Durrow, happy in my own dear land.

• • •

•

I remember the sound of the wind, rustling through the elm tree leaves—its music delighting my ears.

I remember the blackbird cry, flapping its wings in the wind, its song delighting my ears.

I remember the call of the cuckoo in the bright mornings of spring, its call delighting my ears.

I remember the cattle lowing, I remember the great stags leaping, I remember the rivers babbling.

In truth I loved that land, I loved its rain, its sun. Oh, to die in my home!

•COLUMBA'S ROCK•

Delightful it is to stand on the peak of a rock, in the bosom of the isle, gazing on the face of the sea.

I hear the heaving waves chanting a tune to God in heaven; I see their glittering surf.

I see the golden beaches, their sands sparkling; I hear the joyous shrieks of the swooping gulls.

I hear the waves breaking, crashing on rocks, like thunder in heaven. I see the mighty whales.

I watch the ebb and flow of the ocean tide; it holds my secret, my mournful flight from Eire.

Contrition fills my heart as I hear the sea; it chants my sins, sins too numerous to confess.

Let me bless almighty God, whose power extends over sea and land, whose angels watch over all.

Let me study sacred books to calm my soul; I pray for peace, kneeling at heaven's gates.

Let me do my daily work, gathering seaweed, catching fish, giving food to the poor.

Let me say my daily prayers, sometimes chanting, sometimes quiet, always thanking God.

Delightful it is to live on a peaceful isle, in a quiet cell, serving the King of kings.

* * *

One day, when Columba was visiting the graveyard in Iona, he saw an old woman cutting nettles.

"Why are you cutting nettles?" asked Columba.

"Dear father," she replied, "I have only one cow, and it has not yet born a calf. So in the meantime I am living on soup made from nettles."

As he walked on, Columba decided that he too should eat only nettle soup. "If this woman eats nettles in expectation of a calf," he thought, "then I too must surely eat nettles in expectation of God's kingdom." So when he returned to the monastery, he ordered the monk who prepared food to give him nettle soup in future.

The monk was anxious that such a meagre diet would kill their beloved abbot. So he made a special stick, hollow in the middle, for stirring the soup. And as he stirred Columba's soup he secretly poured milk through the stick.

◆　◆　◆

◆

Far from becoming ill, Columba thrived on nettle soup, little knowing that it was laced with milk. Soon he was urging other monks to follow his example; and, seeing how healthy Columba looked, many were eager to try his strange diet. The poor monk in the kitchen now had to make a huge cauldron of nettle soup, pouring milk secretly through his stick.

After a few days the monastery ran out of milk, and the monk had no choice but to confess his trick to Columba. For a moment Columba's face went red with anger; then it broke into uproarious laughter.

"It is God's joke against me," Columba said. "It was only pride that made me tell others of my diet—so I deserve to be tricked."

And he ordered that from then onwards all the monks on Iona should eat proper, nutritious meals.

◆ THE DEATH OF COLUMBA ◆

One day in the second week of May (597) Columba, weary with age, was taken on a wagon to the western part of Iona to visit the brethren working in the fields. He said to them: "During the Easter festival this last April, I greatly desired to depart to Christ the Lord. But I prayed that my departure from this world would be delayed, so that the festival of joy should not be turned for you into a time of sorrow." The monks were very upset when they heard these sad words, and Columba tried to console them. Then, still sitting in the wagon, he turned to face eastwards, and bless the island and all the brethren living there.

At the end of the same week, on the Saturday, the old man and his devoted attendant Diormit went to bless the granary. When Columba had blessed both the building and two heaps of grain that were stored in it, he gave thanks, saying: "I congratulate my family of monks because this year, if I have to depart from them, they shall have ample bread to eat."

Then Columba left the granary, and set off back towards the monastery. About midway along the road he sat down at the place where now a cross has been erected, fixed in a millstone. And while he rested his old bones, the white horse, which carried the milk churns between the pasture and the monastery, came up to him. The horse laid its head on Columba's breast and began to whinny, and even to weep and foam at the mouth—for it seemed to know that its master was about to die. Diormit, seeing this, began to drive away the weeping mourner. But Columba forbade him, saying, "Let him alone, for he loves me. Let him pour out his tears of grief here in my bosom. You, a man with a rational soul, can know nothing about my departure except what I tell you. But this dumb creature, possessing no reason, has been told by the Creator himself that I am about to leave him." So he blessed his servant the horse; and the horse turned sadly away.

Columba then climbed the small hill that overlooks the monastery. And, after he had stood for a while at the top, he raised both his hands and blessed the monastery, saying:

* * *

"On this place, small and poor though it is, the kings of people of these lands will bestow great honour."

He now returned to his cell in the monastery, where he spent the night sitting up on the bare stone which served as his bed. There he dictated to Diormit his last commands to his brethren: "I give to you, my children, these final words. Be at peace with one another, bound together by mutual and unfeigned love. If you do this, according to the example of the ancient fathers, God, who gives strength to the righteous, will bless you; and I, abiding with him, shall intercede for you. Not only will God provide all the things needed for this present life, but he shall prepare for you the blessings of eternity."

After this, as the happy hour of his death approached, Columba fell silent. Then, when the bell began to toll at midnight, he quickly rose and hastened to the church, running faster than the other monks, so that he was the first to enter. He went up to the altar and fell on his knees in prayer. At that moment

Diormit, who was following more slowly, saw from a distance the whole church filled with angelic light. As he reached the door of the church the light faded.

Diormit cried out, his voice choking with tears, "Where are you, where are you, Father?" and groping in the darkness he found Columba lying before the altar. He raised him up a little, and, sitting beside him, laid his head on his lap. Meanwhile the other monks, carrying their lights, arrived, and began to weep at the sight of their dying father. Columba, his soul still present, opened his eyes and looked around him, his face smiling with joy. Diormit lifted Columba's right hand in order to bless the monks; and Columba responded, moving his hand as much as he was able. And so, although his voice was now silent, he could still give his blessing with his hand. As soon as he had given the sign of heavenly benediction, he breathed out his spirit.

When his soul had left the tabernacle of his body, his face remained so ruddy and joyful, gladdened by the vision of the angels com-

◆ ◆ ◆

◆

ing to receive him, that he seemed not to be dead, but only sleeping. And the whole church resounded with cries of grief.

• A TRIBUTE TO COLUMBA •

As long as I lived under Columba's care, I was guarded by the angels of heaven. I could tread the path of fear, because I had a leader who gave me courage.

It was not on a soft bed that he kept his nightly vigils. It was not for his own sins that his body was crucified on the blue waves.

He turned away from Eire, he crossed the rough sea where whales have their sanctuary, he cut through the waves that pressed against him, he attacked the mountains of the sea.

He fought bitter battles with the flesh, he armed himself with the wisdom of the spiritual masters. When he hoisted his sails and crossed the sea, a kingdom was his reward.

Let us give thanks that the wild winds blew Columba to us. Columba, the light of Eire—

there was never before such a noble spirit within a mortal body.

Those who joined his priestly army are bold and brave, moving across the land as angelic warriors. He is their ears when they are deaf, their strength when they are sick, their eyes when they are blind.

I shall always sing of Columba, and ask him to pray for me. In every danger I shall call on him, with all my strength I shall praise him.

May our dear Columba, spiritual conqueror of kings, and gracious father to the humblest peasant, always protect us with his power.

AIDAN AND OSWALD

Aidan is the most famous product of Columba's rigorous regime at Iona; yet the contrast between these two great men could hardly be sharper. Where Columba was stern, making the highest demands of his followers, Aidan was gentle, happy to feed people "spiritual milk"; where Columba was a shrewd political operator, Aidan was guileless and humble, winning kings and peasants by his joyful faith. The story of Aidan's mission to Northumbria, at the invitation of the pious King Oswald, is one of the highlights of Bede's Ecclesiastical History of the English People.

◆ SPIRITUAL MILK ◆

When King Oswald asked the monks of Iona to send a bishop to teach the faith of Christ to himself and his people, they first sent a man of the most austere disposition. But he met with no success among the English, who refused to listen to him. So he returned home, reporting to his brethren that he had been unable to achieve anything amongst such an obstinate and barbarous people. The monks met to debate the wisest course of action, grieving that the English had rejected their preacher, yet still eager to save them. Aidan, who was present at the conference, said to the priest whose efforts had failed: "Brother, it seems to me that you were too severe with your ignorant hearers. You should have followed the example of the apostles, who began by giving people the milk of simple teaching, gradually nourishing them with the Word of God until they were capable of greater perfection, and so could follow the more demanding precepts of Christ."

At this the faces and eyes of all of the conference turned towards Aidan, paying close attention to what he said; and they realised that he was the right person to send as bishop to instruct the ignorant and superstitious people, since he was particularly endowed with the grace of discretion, the mother of all virtues.

Aidan taught the English people by his own holy example. He neither sought nor cared for any worldly possessions, but loved to give away to the poor whatever he had received from kings and chiefs. Whether in town or in the countryside, he travelled on foot, never on horseback unless compelled by some urgent necessity. And as he walked along he stopped and spoke to whomever he met, both rich and poor: if they were heathen, he invited them to embrace the mystery of the faith, and be baptised; and if they were already believers, he strengthened their faith, inspiring them by word and action to be good and generous to their neighbours.

Those who travelled with Aidan, whether

monks or lay folk, were required to meditate, that is, to either read the Scriptures or learn the psalms. This was their daily occupation wherever they went. And if, on special occasions, Aidan was invited to dine with the king, he took with him one or two priests; and when he had eaten only a small amount, he left as soon as possible to read or pray with them. Many men and women at that time, following his example, adopted the custom of fasting on Wednesday and Friday, until three o'clock in the afternoon, throughout the year except during the fifty days after Easter. If wealthy people did wrong, he never kept silent out of fear, but spoke to them frankly. Nor did he try to influence people by offering money, although he often welcomed people to share his meals. Instead, if the wealthy ever gave him money, he either distributed it to the poor, or used it to ransom those who had been sold into slavery. Many of these ransomed slaves became his followers, and he trained them as priests.

Such then was the bishop who preached the Christian faith to King Oswald and the English people under his rule. And, having received the faith, which had been unknown to his ancestors, Oswald was granted by almighty God a kingdom far larger than they had enjoyed: he brought under his sceptre all the provinces of Britain speaking the four languages, British, Pictish, Scottish and English. Yet, even at the height of his power, Oswald remained remarkably humble, as well as kind and generous to the poor and to strangers.

One Easter Oswald invited Aidan to dine with him. A lavish meal, set on a silver dish, was brought to them; and Aidan was about to raise his hand to bless the food, when a servant came in to tell the king that a great crowd of needy folk had gathered outside, begging alms of the king. Oswald immediately ordered the food to be given to the poor, and the silver dish to be broken in pieces and distributed amongst them. Aidan, sitting beside him, was so moved at such generosity that he took hold of the king's hand, and exclaimed, "May this hand never wither." Later events proved that this prayer was heard: when Oswald was killed in battle, his hand and arm were cut off from his body, and they remain uncorrupted to this day.

◆ THE FINE HORSE ◆

One day the king gave to Aidan a very fine horse, in order that he could ride whenever he had to cross a river or undertake a difficult or urgent journey. Soon afterwards, when Aidan was travelling through the countryside, he met a poor man who begged for help. Aidan immediately dismounted and ordered the horse, with all its royal trappings, to be given to the beggar—for he was always compassionate, a friend to the poor and a father to the wretched.

When this story came to the king's ears, he asked Aidan, as they were going into dinner: "My Lord Bishop, why did you give away the royal horse which was so necessary for your use? Have we not many other less valuable horses that are good enough for the poor, without giving away a horse that I had specially selected for you?" The bishop immediately replied: "What are you saying, Your Majesty? Is that foal of a mare more valuable to you than the poor child of God to whom I gave it?" At this they went into dinner, and the bishop sat down in his place; but the king, who had come in from hunting, stood warming himself by the fire, reflecting on what Aidan had said. Suddenly he unbuckled his sword, handing it to a servant, and threw himself down at the bishop's feet, begging forgiveness. "I will never speak of this matter again," he cried; "and nor will I enquire what gifts from me you hand on to God's children." Aidan was deeply moved at this sight; and, standing up himself, he raised the king to his feet, assuring him of his highest regard, and asking him to enjoy the meal without regrets.

•AIDAN'S DEATH•

Aidan frequently used to stay at the king's various country houses, from which he would walk to the surrounding villages to preach the gospel. It was while staying at such a house, near the royal capital, that Aidan fell ill. Near the house was a church, and a tent was erected for Aidan against one of its wooden buttresses. Aidan could thus lean against the buttress, praying, and it was in that position that he died. He had been bishop for sixteen years.

CUTHBERT'S KINGDOM

Cuthbert caught Bede's imagination, prompting him to devote an entire book to his life. The stories of Cuthbert's boisterous childhood, of his nightly vigils amongst the otters at Melrose, and of his humane rule at Lindisfarne portray him as a worthy successor of the gentle Aidan. But it was his retreat to the Farne Islands, where he reigned as "monarch" amongst the birds, which has for centuries caught the popular imagination. His shrine at Durham, where his bones were eventually laid to rest, continues to attract tens of thousands of pilgrims.

•CUTHBERT'S BOYHOOD•

Up to the age of eight Cuthbert was interested in nothing except sports. He enjoyed the company of other children, joining in all their pranks. He was naturally agile and quick-witted, so he usually won whatever games he played; and he was so strong that, when everyone else was exhausted, he was still fresh, looking round triumphantly to see if anyone was willing to challenge him again. He boasted that he had beaten all the children of his age, as well as many older boys, at wrestling, running and jumping.

One day he was playing in a field with a large crowd of other lads, twisting their limbs in all sorts of contortions in the excitement of the game, when a child, apparently no more than three years old, ran up to him. This little boy spoke to Cuthbert with the gravity of an old man, scolding him for wasting his time on idle games, when he should be learning to control his body and mind in the service of God. At first Cuthbert laughed at such an idea, so the little boy burst into tears and threw himself on the ground. The other lads rushed up to console him, asking him why he was crying, but to no avail. Then Cuthbert himself

* * *

◆

tried to console him. The little boy stared Cuthbert straight in the eye: "Why are you so stubborn," the boy blurted out, "persisting in such stupid games, when your own nature is calling you to serve God? You merely make a fool of yourself."

Cuthbert was stunned. He embraced the little boy, who immediately stopped weeping. Cuthbert knew that the boy's words had reached the depths of his heart.

◆ CUTHBERT'S VISION ◆

As Cuthbert grew older he went to work as a shepherd in the hills. One night, when his companions had gone to sleep, he suddenly saw a shaft of light piercing the dark sky, and reaching right down to earth.

The next day he learnt that, at that very moment, Aidan, the beloved bishop of Lindisfarne, had died and been taken up to heaven. Cuthbert immediately took the sheep in his care to their owner, and decided to become a monk—travelling to join the monastery at Melrose.

◆　◆　◆

◆

As a monk Cuthbert was constantly busy, both within and outside the monastery. He was devout in his prayers, and also travelled frequently around the neighbourhood to convert the people from their foolish ways to the wisdom of Christ. Many, who had once held the faith, were now profaning it by wicked deeds; and, when a plague was raging, they forgot the sacred mysteries of Christ into which they had been baptised, and reverted instead to idolatry, seeking protection by magical incantations and bracelets. Cuthbert tirelessly visited the homes of such people, sometimes travelling on horseback, but more usually on foot, to rescue them from their errors.

It was the custom at this time that, when a priest or monk came to a village, the people would gather round to meet him. Such was Cuthbert's skill in teaching, and so gentle and attractive was his personality, that people had no wish to hide from him the secrets of their hearts, but willingly confessed their sins openly. And they would happily try to put

◆ ◆ ◆

◆

into practise the teachings of Christ, which Cuthbert expressed so clearly.

◆CUTHBERT AND THE OTTERS◆

Cuthbert used to rise in the middle of the night, while all the other monks were sleeping, to go out alone and pray, returning to the monastery just in time for morning worship. One night one of the brethren watched him creep out, secretly following him in order to find out what he did.

Cuthbert went down to the river near the monastery, and waded out into the water until his arms and neck were covered. There he remained, praying and singing for many hours. At dawn he came out of the river, and knelt on the bank in prayer. Then two otters came out of the water and stretched themselves out beside him, warming his feet with their breath, and drying him by the heat of their bodies. When the otters had finished, Cuthbert blessed them, and they slipped back into the water. Cuthbert then returned home, and joined the other monks in the chapel.

◆ ◆ ◆

◆

But the monk who had spied on him was so frightened and distressed that he could scarcely walk. When he finally reached the monastery, later in the morning, he prostrated himself before Cuthbert, his voice choking with tears, and begged Cuthbert's forgiveness. "What is wrong, what have you done?" Cuthbert asked; "have you been spying on my night's labours? I will forgive you—so long as you tell nobody about it while I am still alive."

•CUTHBERT AND LINDISFARNE•

After Cuthbert had passed many years at Melrose, and distinguished himself by many signs of holiness, he was asked to go to Lindisfarne as prior. His task was to inspire the monks there, many of whom had grown slack, to follow more strictly the Rule laid down by Aidan.

Some of the monks were stubborn, clinging to their lax habits. Cuthbert won them over by gentleness and patience. At chapter meetings the monks frequently hurled bitter insults at him, but he would put an end to argument by calmly rising from his chair, and walking out. The next day he would behave as if nothing had happened, showing to all the brethren the same warm friendship. Though he was often overwhelmed with sorrow at the laxness and the conflicts within the monastery, outwardly he was always cheerful. And soon it was clear to all the monks that it was the Holy Spirit who gave him strength to endure the attacks against him. So within a few years all the monks willingly obeyed him.

Such was Cuthbert's love of prayer that he often stayed awake for three or four nights in a row, without even lying down on his bed, in order to worship God. And during the day he shared fully in the manual work of the monastery, as well as visiting all the people on the island. And whenever the heaviness of sleep threatened to overcome him, he would dig more furiously or walk more vigorously. If any monk complained that a restless brother had awakened him at the wrong moment, Cuthbert would scold the monk, saying: "Nobody can annoy me by waking me up; on the contrary, I am pleased because, by driving away sleep, he enables me to do something useful."

Cuthbert wore the simplest clothes, yet was always careful to be clean and tidy. He forbade his monks from wearing expensive dyed cloth, insisting that they should be content with natural wool.

◆CUTHBERT ON FARNE ISLAND◆

After many years in the monastery, Cuthbert desired the greater spiritual joy of living as a hermit; and was delighted that his brethren supported this desire, thinking him worthy of this high calling.

To learn the first steps of the hermit's life he retired to a more secluded place away from the monastery. Then, having fought there for some time against the devil, through solitary prayer and fasting, he decided to seek a more remote battlefield, far away from his fellow men. Thus he rowed out to Farne Island, which is some miles from Lindisfarne across very deep water—and beyond it is the boundless ocean. No-one had ever dwelt on this island before, as it was believed to be haunted by Satan's angels; but Cuthbert was fearless, knowing that with God's power any evil ghosts could be routed.

So this soldier of Christ became monarch of the island, building a city fit for his humble rule. He constructed a circular wall, higher than a man, using rough stones and peat that he found on the island itself. Inside he built a small chapel and a hut in which to live, making the roofs from rough-hewn timber and straw. Down at the landing-place he put up a much larger house for guests. The island was so small that it had no streams: so he dug a pit, which filled with fresh, clear water.

When visitors came, Cuthbert went out from his enclosure to look after them, taking water from the well to wash their feet. And they too insisted that he took off his boots so they could wash his feet. They would find long thick calluses where the boots had rubbed his shins during all his prayers and genuflections.

◆ ◆ ◆

◆

At first Cuthbert depended on bread brought by visitors. But he wanted to follow the example of the desert fathers, living by the labour of his own hands. So he asked his brethren to bring over tools to dig the soil, and seeds of wheat to sow.

He planted the seeds in spring, but by midsummer nothing had grown. "It is either the nature of this land or the will of God," Cuthbert said to his brethren; "but, whatever the reason, wheat will not grow here. Bring me barley instead to see if that will flourish here. If God does not let that yield a harvest, I would rather return to the monastery than continue living off others."

The monks brought barley, and Cuthbert sowed it long after the proper time. Yet it soon sprang forth, giving an abundant crop. However, just as it began to ripen, some birds flew down, and began devouring it. Cuthbert came out from his hut to speak to them. "Why are you eating crops which you did not sow?"

he asked. "Is it that your need is greater than mine? If so, you have God's permission to help yourselves; but if not, go away, and stop damaging what does not belong to you."

The birds flew off, and Cuthbert harvested the barley. But some time later the birds returned, and began taking straw from the roof of the guest-house to use in building their nests. Cuthbert came out and shouted at them: "In the name of Christ, depart at once; do not dare remain to cause further damage." Scarcely had he finished speaking than the birds had flown away, their heads bowed in shame.

Three days later one of the birds returned. Cuthbert was digging, and the bird landed in front of him, his feathers ruffled and his head drooping right down to his feet, as if to beg the saint's forgiveness. Cuthbert was overjoyed, happily forgiving all the birds, and inviting them to return. Back they came, carrying a gift—a lump of pig's lard. Cuthbert kept it in the guest-house, inviting visitors to grease their shoes with it. "If even the birds can show such humility and kindness," Cuthbert would say, "how much more we humans should seek such virtues."

The birds remained on the island with Cuthbert for many years, building their nests from materials which they themselves had gathered.

◆ CUTHBERT AS BISHOP ◆

Numerous people came to see Cuthbert on Farne Island, not just from Lindisfarne but from every area of Britain. They confessed their sins and opened their hearts to him, telling him all their anxieties and problems, in the hope of receiving guidance and comfort. They were never disappointed: everyone who came felt their worries lifted from their shoulders, and those whose hearts were chilled by sadness found warmth in Cuthbert's words. Whenever people expressed admiration for his way of life, he replied that it was far easier to live alone than in a monastery or a family: "Within a community you must learn obedience to the will of others, which is the hardest virtue of all."

But Cuthbert was, on one further occasion, forced to submit to others. When the old bishop of Lindisfarne died, a great synod met, and, by unanimous consent, chose Cuthbert to replace him. A number of priests and chieftains rowed out to Farne Island to beg Cuthbert to accept the yoke of episcopacy. At first Cuthbert refused. But they persisted, their eyes filled with tears. At last Cuthbert agreed, and they took him back to the synod, where he was consecrated.

As bishop Cuthbert decided to follow strictly the example of the apostles. He protected the people committed to his charge by his constant prayers for them, and he guided them, not by giving advice, but by the example of his own holy life. He visited those who were sad or depressed; he persuaded the rich to give food to the hungry and clothes to the destitute. He also took delight in living simply and keeping the monastic rule amidst the pomp of the world.

* * *

• CUTHBERT'S DEATH •

After he had been bishop for only two years, Cuthbert decided to return to Farne Island. His brethren from Lindisfarne gathered at the shore, amongst them, an old monk, who asked him: "Tell us, when shall we see you again?" Cuthbert replied: "When you bring back my corpse."

For two months Cuthbert rediscovered the joys of a hermit's life, and took pleasure in adapting once again to his old routine. Then suddenly he was struck by a severe pain in his stomach, as if a fire was burning inside him. On that very day a priest from Lindisfarne arrived by boat. So Cuthbert, who knew he was dying, dictated his final instructions to his brethren.

"Always live in peace with one another. When you meet to discuss your common affairs, you must aim to reach a unanimous decision. Live at peace also with your neighbours, never treating others with contempt, but always welcoming them into the monastery. Never imagine that your way of life is superior to that of men and women in the world: all who share the Christian faith are equal in God's sight. Your duty is simply to follow the rules of monastic life which our forefathers laid down."

After he had finished speaking he lapsed into silence, and remained perfectly still until evening. Then the priest administered the eucharist. As Cuthbert swallowed the bread and wine, he lifted his arms above his head, as if to embrace an angel of God. Then, his face filled with joy, he breathed his last.

HILDA AND CAEDMON

The story of Hilda, the royal abbess of Whitby whose intellect was admired by scholars throughout Britain, and Caedmon, the lowly cowherd who composed exquisite religious ballads, has been related to countless generations of children. Hilda was the last great Celtic saint, hosting the Synod of Whitby which spelled the victory of Catholic over Celt. But as patron of popular bards like Caedmon she kept alive one of the finest traditions of the Celtic church. Sadly only a fragment of Caedmon's poetry survives, that contained in Bede's history.

• THE MIGHTY ABBESS •

Hilda was born of royal blood, the daughter of Hereric who was himself the nephew of King Edwin.

As a young woman she decided to abandon the secular life and devote herself wholly to God. At first she went to East Anglia, where the king was a relative; and she intended to travel on to France, giving up her home and all worldly possessions, in order to live as an exile for Christ. However, after a year, Aidan called her home, giving her land on the north bank of the River Wear to found a monastery. She lived there for a further year; but only a few others came to join her. So Aidan sent her to Hartlepool, to become abbess of a monastery which had been started a few years earlier. There she imposed a regular pattern of work and prayer, according to the example of the early fathers; and Aidan and other devout people frequently visited her, admiring her innate wisdom.

When she had been at this monastery for some years she undertook to create a new monastery at Whitby. There she established the same pattern of work and prayer. And, following the example of the primitive church, everything was held in common, with no personal property, so that people were neither rich nor poor, but all had sufficient. Her wisdom was so great that kings and princes, as well as ordinary folk, came to ask her advice; and she urged all who visited to read the Scriptures, and always to be generous to those in need.

• THE LOWLY COWHERD •

In the monastery at Whitby there lived a brother, Caedmon, who was supremely gifted in composing religious songs: whenever a passage out of Scripture was explained to him, he would turn it into a sweet and joyful ballad in his native tongue. These songs have inspired many to reject the ways of the world, and follow the path of Christ. Others after him have tried to compose devotional songs, but none could compare with him, for he learnt his art from God himself; and so he could never compose trivial or frivolous songs, but only those which spoke of God's love. Indeed, while he was still living in the world, he refused to use his gift for mere amusement:

at feasts, where people took it in turns to entertain each other with bawdy songs, he would slip away from the table and go home.

It was after one such feast that Caedmon had a strange dream. As the entertainment began he left the house, and went out to the stables where he was employed to tend the animals. When his work was over, he lay down on his bed; and in his sleep a man appeared to him, calling him by name: "Caedmon," the man said, "sing me a song." "I cannot sing," replied Caedmon; "that is why I left the feast and came out here." "But," the man persisted, "you shall sing to me." "What shall I sing about?" asked Caedmon. "Sing about the creation of the world." So Caedmon began to sing verses that he had never heard before, in praise of God:

Now must we praise the guardian of
heaven,
The power of conception of the law,
And all his works, as he, eternal Lord,
Father of glory, started every wonder.

❖ ❖ ❖

❖

First he created heaven as a roof,
The holy Maker, for the sons of men.
Then the eternal keeper of mankind
Furnished the earth below, the land for
    men,
Almighty God and everlasting Lord.

When Caedmon awoke he remembered
everything that he had sung in his dream, and
soon added more verses in the same style to
complete the song. Then he went to the steward of the estate, who, having heard the song,
took him to abbess Hilda. She asked him, in
the presence of many learned men, to recount
his dream, and sing the song, so that they
could judge its quality and origin. They all
agreed that Caedmon's dream came from
God. Then they read to him a passage of
Scripture, asking him to turn it into a ballad.
The next morning he returned, having turned
the passage into a most beautiful song. Hilda
was overjoyed that God had bestowed such
an extraordinary gift on so humble a man, and

she urged him to give up his secular occupation, and join the monastery.

She then ordered those brethren who could read to teach Caedmon all the stories and teachings of the Bible. And Caedmon, reflecting on what he had heard like a cow chewing the cud, turned the Scripture passages into joyful songs. He sang of the creation of the world, the origins of the human race, the Hebrews' exodus from Egypt, and their entry into the promised land, as well as of the Lord's birth, death, resurrection and ascension into heaven.

•HILDA'S DEATH•

When Hilda had governed the monastery at Whitby for many years, it pleased God to test her soul by a long sickness, in order that, following the apostle's example, her strength might be made perfect in weakness. She was attacked by a burning fever that racked her continually for six years; but during this time she never ceased to give thanks to her Maker, nor to instruct the flock committed to her charge, both privately and publicly. Thus, just as she had shown people when in health how to serve God obediently, now she demonstrated how to be grateful to God in trouble and sickness. In the seventh year of her sickness the fever penetrated deep into her body, and she knew her end was near. At about cockcrow she received the eucharist to help her on her journey through death; then she summoned her brothers and sisters to her side, urging them always to live in peace, both amongst themselves and with all around them. And while she was still speaking, she joyfully embraced death.

ILTUT'S SCHOOL

The patron saint of Wales, David, was himself a pupil of Iltut; and it is the latter who should properly be regarded as the founder of the Welsh church. Iltut came to Wales as a soldier of fortune from Brittany, and, according to the ancient "record" of his life, fought briefly as a knight in King Arthur's army. But it was while serving the king of Glamorgan that he encountered a Christian hermit, Cadoc, and was converted to the faith. His school on the south Glamorgan coast attracted the sons of kings and chiefs from throughout Wales, sending them back to convert their own tribes. In addition to David, who was the son of a chieftain from the western tip of Wales, Iltut's most famous pupil was Samson, who went to Iltut's own native land of Brittany to establish the church there.

◆　◆　◆

◆

Iltut's parents wanted their son to be a cultured and learned man. So they sent him to the best teachers, and he proved the most able and intelligent pupil in both the arts and the sciences.

But once he was grown up, Iltut's only desire was to become a soldier, and fight glorious battles. He had heard of the great bravery of King Arthur, so he sailed across the Channel to offer his services to this noble warrior. King Arthur received him graciously, but Iltut soon realised there were already so many fine knights in King Arthur's court that a young soldier like himself would have no chance to excel.

So he travelled onwards to Glamorgan, where he was welcomed by King Paulinus. The king was delighted to have such an educated and pretty man in his court, and soon appointed him to be steward of the royal household. Then, after Iltut had shown his prowess in battle, the king promoted him to be chief over his army.

❖ ❖ ❖

❖

One day Iltut took a group of knights hunting. They went to the forest where the venerable old hermit Cadoc lived. Iltut became separated from the others; and, when the others approached Cadoc's hut, they sent a message demanding food and drink, threatening to take it by force if Cadoc refused their request. Cadoc replied by inviting them into his hut for a meal, which he himself cooked and served. The knights treated Cadoc like the meanest slave, and during the meal told obscene jokes, in the hope of making Cadoc lose his temper. But Cadoc simply smiled at their folly.

Iltut eventually arrived at the hut himself. And when he saw what his knights were doing, he was horrified. He took out his sword, and drove them out, threatening to kill anyone who spoke another word to the hermit. The cowardly knights ran off into the forest. Iltut then returned to Cadoc, fell on his knees, and begged forgiveness for his knights' behaviour. Cadoc bent down and lifted Iltut to his feet, warmly embracing him.

◆ ◆ ◆

That night, as Iltut lay awake in bed, his heart was filled with love for the old hermit: the life of such a man, who was victorious in battle with Satan, seemed so much finer than that of a soldier, whose only battles were with other soldiers. Then, when he had fallen asleep, an angel came and spoke to Iltut in a dream: "Until now you have been a knight serving mortal kings; from now on I want you to be a knight in the service of an immortal king, the King of all kings."

At dawn the following morning Iltut crept out of the royal palace, leaving behind his sword and armour, and wearing only a rough woollen cloak. His heart was filled with both joy and fear, as he set out to join God's army: he knew that the war against Satan is far harder than any human wars, but the rewards far greater.

• ILTUT'S MONASTERY •

Iltut walked southwards to the coast, and came to a wide flat valley, with steep cliffs on either side, running down to the beach. Iltut could see the ground was fertile, and that the river would provide ample water. So he built himself a hut, and for the next three months learnt how to pray. He fed on wild roots and fruit, but also cleared the land round his hut and sowed seed.

One day a stag appeared in the valley, galloping as fast as it could, and bounded into Iltut's hut while he was inside praying. A few moments later a pack of hounds arrived, barking wildly. But as soon as they reached the hut the hounds fell silent, and stood quite still, with their heads bowed. Finally King Paulinus and his knights rode up, and started yelling at the hounds, ordering them to go into the hut to kill the stag. But the hounds remained motionless.

Then Iltut emerged from the hut, and welcomed King Paulinus and the knights. They were so astonished to see him that for a full minute they were speechless. At last the king erupted, his face ablaze with anger, accusing Iltut of betraying him. The knights joined in the accusations, drawing their swords and pointing them at Iltut. Iltut—like Cadoc facing similar insults—simply smiled, and invited them into his hut for a meal. And at that moment the stag poked his head out of the hut, and looked plaintively at the king.

The accusations melted on the king's lips: he slowly climbed down from his horse, and followed Iltut into the hut. The knights too came inside, and Iltut invited the whole group to sit in a circle. As it was so crowded, Iltut led the stag out, and throughout the meal the stag and the hounds lay down quietly outside. Iltut then served the king and knights with the wild roots he had gathered that day.

At the end, the king knelt before Iltut and begged forgiveness. Iltut bent down and lifted up the king, embracing him warmly. Then the king asked if he could send his son to Iltut to be educated. Iltut gladly agreed.

Soon Iltut's valley near the sea became the largest school in the whole of Britain. Kings and chiefs from the whole country sent their children there; and numerous other monks

◆　◆　◆

◆

came to share in Iltut's great work. Two of Iltut's pupils became bishops: David, who founded a monastery in the far west of Wales, and converted the tribal people in that area; and Samson, who sailed to Brittany and spread the gospel there.

Iltut firmly believed that intellectual education must be mixed with hard manual work, and that monks and pupils should grow the food they eat. So everyone had to spend four hours each day working outside, and within a few years the whole valley had been cleared for farming. Iltut invented a new plough which doubled the speed at which land could be prepared, so farmers too came to the valley to see and copy this implement. Iltut would only show them the plough if they agreed to listen to the gospel.

Thus Iltut taught both royal households and humble peasants the truths of Christ.

◆ILTUT'S ESCAPE◆

After many years King Paulinus died. But the son whom Iltut educated did not succeed to

◆ ◆ ◆

◆

the throne; instead a cruel warrior, Merchion, seized the crown, exiling the rightful heir.

Iltut by now was the most famous person in the whole kingdom, and greatly loved by all people. So Merchion regarded Iltut as a threat to his power, and decided to kill him. He planned to attack the monastery at night, and slay Iltut with his own sword. But a few hours before the attack was due, one of Merchion's knights, who secretly admired Iltut, sent a messenger to Iltut to warn him.

Far from being afraid, Iltut saw this as a message from God, prompting him to give up his busy life as abbot, and withdraw to a remote cave in order to devote himself wholly to prayer. So Iltut, without telling anyone, crept out of the monastery—just as, many years earlier, he had crept out of the royal palace—and set off westwards along the coast. Eventually he reached a beautiful golden beach at the end of a long peninsula; and beside the beach was a cave which Iltut made his home. A flat rock served as a bed, and the seagulls were his companions. He allowed his hair and beard to grow, so that passing travellers would be unable to recognise him. The monks in the meantime had been scouring the countryside, but eventually with heavy hearts they decided that their beloved abbot had left them forever.

However, about a year later, a monk was travelling from Iltut's old monastery to the new monastery which David had established on the far western tip of Wales. The monk was carrying a brass bell as a gift for David, and took a wrong turning so he came near to Iltut's cave. Iltut heard the sweet sound of the bell, and came out to see what was happening. Iltut simply struck the bell three times and returned to his cave. The monk just smiled, not recognising his old abbot, and went on his way. But from that moment the bell stopped ringing.

When the monk finished his journey, he presented the bell to David, telling the story of how it had stopped ringing. David was overjoyed. "Now at last," he exclaimed, "God has told us where our beloved Father Iltut is hiding." David sent a group of monks to Iltut's cave, to plead with Iltut to return to his monastery. Iltut refused to go, so monks stayed with him, caring for him and praying with him until he died.

SAINTS AND BEASTS

The Celtic Christians saw the beauties of nature as our mirror on to the glories of heaven. Their literature is rich in stories of saints making friends with animals, birds and insects. It was a hound and a robin who led Mungo to build his monastery where Glasgow cathedral now stands—so the three of them together are the founders of that great city. It was a wild boar, a fox, a badger, a wolf and a doe who joined Piran to form the first monastery in Cornwall, and then helped Piran convert the Cornish people. It was a cow who attracted monks to join Kevin in Glendalough in Ireland, and blackbirds who were his companions when he later became a hermit. And it was a cock, a mouse and a fly that taught the hermit Colman how to pray.

Mungo knew that God was calling him to found a new monastery amongst the pagan tribesmen of Scotland, to bear witness to the love of Christ. So he set out from home in search of a suitable place.

Soon a wild hound appeared, and began to lead him. The hound took him over steep mountains, into deep valleys, and through dark forests. Each night Mungo and the hound lay down in the grass next to one another; and before they fell asleep they talked to each other, Mungo speaking in words, and the hound replying with barks and growls.

Eventually they arrived at a beautiful lush valley, with a clear blue river running through it. Around the valley they could see little columns of smoke, so they knew there were many tribal people living there. The hound stopped near the riverbank, and began scratching the ground with its feet, tearing up tufts of grass. Mungo fell to his knees, asking God whether this was truly the place to build his monastery.

At that moment a little robin flew down from

a tree, landing on Mungo's shoulder. It flapped its wings, and, with its little beak, kissed Mungo on the neck. Mungo knew that, if even the birds welcomed him, this was the place to found his monastery. The hound went off to collect branches, and the bird brought leaves and grass; and soon Mungo had built himself a hut.

Then the hound came up to Mungo and growled loudly, bowing its head. Mungo realised it wanted a blessing; so he laid his hand on its head, and prayed for God's guidance on it. The hound then went off and in the following days and months sent other men to join Mungo, all of whom had also felt called to start a new monastery. And the robin and the hound helped each one to build himself a hut.

As the community grew, the local people came to visit it, wanting to see their new neighbours. When they learnt that the newcomers were Christian, the local people recalled the great Ninian who had visited them many years earlier; and they gave thanks that

God had sent another apostle to live amongst them. Mungo and his brethren gladly welcomed the sick into their community, nursing them back to health, and shared their simple food with hungry travellers. Within a few years Mungo's monastery was renowned in the whole area for its generosity and kindness to all in need. And many people embraced the gospel which inspired that unassuming love.

◆ PIRAN'S ANIMAL MONASTERY ◆

When Piran first arrived in Cornwall, he sat down under a tree; and lying under the same tree was a wild boar. At first, on seeing Piran, the boar fled in terror. But then, sensing Piran's great love for all God's creatures, the boar became tame, and returned to Piran to become his servant. He thus became Piran's first monk. The boar began to tear branches and grass with his teeth, and built Piran a simple cell in which to live. And soon other animals came out of the forest to join Piran and the boar: a fox, a badger, a wolf and a doe. They were all quite tame, obeying Piran as their abbot.

◆ ◆ ◆

◆

One day the fox, who was more crafty than the other animals, stole Piran's shoes; and, abandoning his intention to live as a monk, he carried them to his old lair in the forest, to chew them there. Piran, when he realised what had happened, sent the badger after the fox, to persuade him to return to the monastery. So the badger, who knew the forest well, went straight to the fox's lair; and, seeing the fox about to eat his master's shoes, bit his ears and tail. Then, with his teeth in the fox's fur, the badger pulled the fox back to the monastery.

When the fox arrived, Piran asked him: "Why have you committed this crime, dear brother—something that a monk should never do? Look, we all share the same sweet water and the same food. And if you had craved meat, according to your nature, God would have turned the bark of this tree into meat for you." The fox begged Piran's forgiveness, and did penance by fasting, refusing to eat until Piran gave permission.

And from then onwards all the animals lived

◆ ◆ ◆

◆

in peace, bound together by devotion to their abbot.

⬧KEVIN AND THE COW⬧

Walking alone through remote regions of Ireland, Kevin came one day to a valley, with a beautiful, clear stream running down the mountains into two blue lakes. Kevin decided to stay near the lower lake, drinking its water, gathering herbs to eat from round its shore, and sleeping in the hollow of an old tree nearby.

Some nearby herdsmen took their cows to graze each day in this valley. Since God wanted to reveal Kevin to other people, he caused one of the cows to visit Kevin daily. The cow would eat the cut grass near Kevin's tree, drink from the lake, and nuzzle up to Kevin, licking his rough clothes; then in the evening, when the cow heard the herdsmen shouting at the cattle to drive them home, she would hurry back to the herd. Every day as the herd entered the valley, the cow would steal away up to Kevin. To the herdsmen's

⬧   ⬧   ⬧

⬧

amazement she began to give abundant milk, far greater in quantity and far richer than that of the other cows. The herdsmen reported this to their master, who said to them: "Keep a close eye on her, and discover the pasture where she grazes."

So the next day one of the herdsmen followed the cow up to the valley to Kevin's tree. And when he saw the cow licking Kevin's clothes he was filled with an irrational anger —as if Kevin's holiness was a judgement on himself. He started to insult Kevin and beat the cow, and finally drove the cow back down the valley, thrashing it with a stick.

That evening at the farm all the cows and calves fell into a frenzy, foaming at the mouth; and the cows became so wild that they began to butt their own calves with their heads. The herdsman who had insulted Kevin ran to his master to say what was happening; and, after questioning the herdsman, the master ordered the herdsman to go to Kevin and seek forgiveness, begging him to heal the cattle. The herdsman ran to the valley, and fell

◆　◆　◆

◆

on his knees before Kevin. Kevin blessed him; then he fetched some water from the lake, and blessed that also, ordering the herdsman to take it to the cows and sprinkle it over them. The herdsman did as Kevin told him, causing the frenzy to cease instantly; and the cows began to lick their calves with love.

And Kevin's fame spread across the whole region.

◆ KEVIN AND THE WILD BOAR ◆

Gradually other men came to join Kevin at the lake, and a large monastery grew up round the tree where Kevin lived. At length Kevin grew weary of the bustle of community life; and, leaving the monastery under the charge of others whom he trusted, Kevin went up the valley for about a mile, building himself a small hut at the top. He ordered the monks not to bring him food, nor to come to him except in dire emergency. For company he had the wild animals, who would come and drink water from his cupped hands. Kevin also constructed out of branches and leaves a small chapel where he could pray.

One day a wild boar came running through the woods, panting with fright, and hid in Kevin's chapel. A few moments later a cruel huntsman called Brandub, notorious for killing both animals and humans merely for pleasure, arrived with a pack of snarling hounds. The hounds went up to the entrance of the chapel, but refused to go in, falling silent and bowing their heads. Brandub was on the point of yelling at the hounds, accusing them of cowardice, when he saw Kevin nearby, standing under a tree; birds were perched on Kevin's arms and were flying round his head, singing with joy. Then a wind arose, and the leaves in the tree became a chorus for the birds' song, rustling in perfect harmony.

The cruel huntsman was filled with fear, and fell off his horse onto the ground. Then he crawled to Kevin, and begged his blessing. From that day onwards Brandub never again killed either people or animals, and lived instead on wild herbs.

♦ ♦ ♦

◆ KEVIN AND THE BLACKBIRD ◆

Kevin devoted part of each day to reading the Scriptures, sitting in his hut, with his arms stretched out through the window reaching up to heaven. One day, while he was reading, a blackbird, thinking the arm was a branch, settled on Kevin's open hand. There it made a nest and laid some eggs.

When Kevin saw what was happening he was so moved by love for the bird that he did not move. Instead he remained in that same position until the eggs were hatched and the young birds could fly.

◆ COLMAN'S TEACHERS ◆

Colman was so eager to imitate the poverty of Christ that he had no property and no earthly possessions whatever—unless his three dearest friends could be called possessions. These friends were a cock, a mouse and a fly.

The cock used to crow in the middle of the night in order to wake Colman for prayer. The mouse would then wake Colman in the morning by gnawing at his clothes and nibbling his ears. Even when Colman was utterly exhausted from his long night vigils, and when his body craved sleep, the mouse kept nibbling until Colman got up—to ensure that Colman never gave in to the sin of sloth.

But the fly's service was the most remarkable. When Colman sat down to read the Scriptures, the fly would walk down the page at precisely the same pace as Colman read the lines. And if Colman was called away on some business, or if he looked up from the page to reflect on what he had read, the fly stayed at the line. Thus when Colman continued reading, he could find his place at once.

At length these three creatures died, so Colman lost their service and companionship. And, his heart heavy with sorrow, he wrote to his spiritual friend, Columba, abbot of Iona. Columba replied both in jest and in wisdom: "To you the cock, the mouse and the fly were as precious as the richest jewels; so rejoice that God has taken those jewels to himself."

MONKS AND
HERMITS

Some of the most popular Celtic verses are by monks
and hermits, celebrating their way of life. The most
striking theme is the unity of man and nature, and
hence the community of all God's creatures. The joy
and cheerfulness of these poems stands in marked contrast to the gloom and solemnity of later medieval
spiritual writings. The poem "Two Hermits in One
House" describes a husband and wife taking monastic
vows, yet still living together as brother and sister; it
was a practice common in the Celtic church, but later
suppressed. The final passage in this section is a description of David's monastery in Wales, and came to
be regarded as David's Rule which was applied in
numerous other communities.

I wish, ancient and eternal King, to live in a hidden hut in the wilderness.

A narrow blue stream beside it, and a clear pool for washing away my sins by the grace of the Holy Spirit.

A beautiful wood all around, where birds of every kind of voice can grow up and find shelter.

Facing southwards to catch the sun, with fertile soil around it suitable for every kind of plant.

And virtuous young men to join me, humble and eager to serve God.

Twelve young men—three fours, four threes, two sixes, six pairs—willing to do every kind of work.

A lovely church, with a white linen cloth over the altar, a home for God from heaven.

A Bible surrounded by four candles, one for each of the gospels.

A special hut in which to gather for meals, talking cheerfully as we eat, without sarcasm, without boasting, without any evil words.

Hens laying eggs for us to eat, leeks growing near the stream, salmon and trout to catch, and bees providing honey.

Enough food and clothing given by our Heavenly King, and enough time to sit and pray to him.

◆A PEACEFUL COMPANY◆

I have a hut in the wood; no-one knows of it except God.

An ash tree grows on one side, a hazel on the other, and a great oak tree overhangs it, sheltering it from wind and rain.

A honeysuckle climbs around its doorposts, and a blackbird nests in the roof, singing a sweet melody.

◆ ◆ ◆

◆

Around my hut are apple trees, yielding the richest fruit. Nearby is a spring, giving the purest water, and beside it watercress sprouts in abundance.

In the wood behind my hut swine, goats, boars and deer graze peacefully together, with a family of badgers alongside them. And foxes come to leap amongst them. Yes, I have the most noble princes for company.

God has sent hens to lay eggs for me, and bees to give me honey. He has planted wild onions around me, and the trees are heavy with succulent berries.

Countless birds come to visit me: wild geese, ducks, before the beginning of winter; fair white birds, cranes, seagulls, singing the songs of the waves; the thrush chanting sweet carols, and in summer the familiar cuckoo above my hut.

All around me the most beautiful music plays: the songs of the birds, the lowing of cattle, the leaves rustling in the wind, the cascade of the river. No king could hire such music with gold; it is the music of Christ himself, given freely.

My pleasures are greater than any wealth could buy. A peaceful company surrounds me, riven by no quarrels or strife, but united by Christ in our midst.

◆GOD'S HOUSE◆

A household full of people could not be more happy than my little oratory in the forest.

It is God who built it: he gave the branches of trees to construct the frame; and to plaster the walls; and grass to thatch the roof.

It is God who dwells there: when I kneel and pray I know he is with me; and when I lie down to sleep I know his angels guard me.

◆HOSPITALITY◆

Whether the sun is at its height, or the moon and stars pierce the darkness, my little hut is always open. It shall never be closed to anyone, lest I should close it to Christ himself.

Whether my guest is rich and noble, or whether he is poor and ragged, my tiny larder is always open. I shall never refuse to share my food, lest the Son of Mary should go hungry.

◆ THE HERMIT AND HIS BLACKBIRD ◆

I need to watch the sun, to calculate the hours that I should pray to God. But the blackbird who nests in the roof of my hut makes no such calculations: he sings God's praises all day long.

I need books to read, to learn the hidden truths of God. But the blackbird who shares my simple meals needs no written texts: he can read the love of God in every leaf and flower.

I need to beg forgiveness, to make myself pure and fit for God. But the blackbird who drinks with me from the stream sheds no tears of contrition: he is as God made him, with no stain of sin.

•THE HERMIT IN A CAVE•

As I look out from my cave, I can see the wide ocean, stretching west, north and south to the ends of the earth.

I watch the sea-birds swoop, and I hear them shriek; and in my mind I can see the ocean depths teeming with fish.

The earth is both majestic and playful, both solemn and joyful; in all this it reflects the One who made it.

•BELLS AND WOMEN•

In the middle of the night the monastery bell awakes me for prayer, its sound carried on the chilly wind.

I would rather follow its call into church than spend the night with a sexy woman.

◆ A TREE ORATORY ◆

My little oratory gives me greater delight than the finest mansion. From it I can watch the sun and the moon move across the sky, and the stars gather like soldiers to guard me at night.

Who made it? God made it. He planted the seed that grew into this mighty tree. And, where the boughs rise out of the trunk, he fashioned a hollow where I can sit.

Who protects me? God protects me. He put branches and leaves above me to shield me from rain. And he put me high above the ground, safe from the spears and swords of robbers.

◆ THE DYING HERMIT ◆

Alone in my little hut in the forest I have prepared for death; without moving I have been on a long journey towards my heavenly home.

I have trodden down my evil passions, stamped upon anger and greed; I have cast aside jealousy and fear, leaving them by the wayside.

At times my pace has been bold and fast along the gospel way; at times I have crawled on bended knee, crying for forgiveness.

Now my journey is almost finished, my Creator comes to fetch me; alone I came to my hut in the forest, and alone in death I shall leave it.

◆ A KING BECOMES A MONK ◆

Let me sharpen my knife, that I may shave my head to honour the great King. Let me give the hair of my head to God, as I make my vow to him.

I will shave my locks in honour of Mary: my hair is strong and dark, a handsome gift for the highest of women.

I have never before cut my own hair: always in the past beautiful girls have cut and combed my royal locks.

◆ ◆ ◆

◆

Now it is Mary herself who is guiding my hands: it is she who is cutting my hair.

Mary, when my head is bare, preserve me from cold and heat: watch over me like the branch of a mighty tree, shielding me from sun, and sheltering me from rain.

•TWO HERMITS IN ONE HOUSE•

When we were young—bashful, yet beautiful—we walked hand in hand across the hills of Ulster, whispering words of love to one another.

I had known you since we were both aged seven, and I had watched you grow into a maiden of rare beauty: to look upon you was like gazing onto heaven itself.

When we married we lived a simple, blameless life, working hard during the day, and enjoying one another at night; I shall always remember the happiness of those early years.

You bore five children, and I toiled in the fields to feed them: I shall always thank God that he provided enough for our needs.

Now our children are adults, our bodies are old and wrinkled, and the taste of pleasure fades; the joys of this world grow less, so the joys of prayer grow greater.

Let us be companions on the pilgrimage of prayer; let us be brother and sister before the altar of God.

As the darkness of age covers our faces, let the light of heaven penetrate our souls.

We shall be two hermits in one house; two souls devoted to one God.

◆ THE RULE OF ST. DAVID ◆

The community built a fine monastery in the place which an angel had shown David. And when it was completed David composed a Rule by which they should live.

Every monk must share in the daily toil, working with his hands. Since idleness is the mother of petty gossip and quarrels, so all must labour so hard that they want only to love one another. They should dig the ground

◆   ◆   ◆

134

◆

with mattocks and shovels, wield hoes to cut weeds and axes to chop wood, and provide for themselves all the necessities of life. They should reject all gifts, and have no personal possessions. There should be no oxen to plough the fields, but each monk should work as an ox, pulling the plough himself. When the manual work is finished there should be no grumblings, and no conversation beyond what is necessary. Instead the monks should return to their cells, to spend the rest of the day reading, writing or praying.

When evening comes, the chapel bell should be struck; and each monk should immediately leave what he is doing—even if he is in the middle of writing a letter—and in silence hasten to the chapel. There the monks should sing the psalms, with heart and voice in perfect harmony; and afterwards remain quietly on their knees until the stars appear in the sky, to announce that the day's work is done.

Then they should walk to the refectory, and assemble round the table to refresh their weary limbs with food. But they should not eat in excess, for even bread, if eaten greedily, induces a selfish spirit. Each should eat only what he needs, according to his age and health. There should not be a variety of dishes to serve different tastes, nor any of the richer foods; instead the monks should have only bread and herbs seasoned with salt, quenching their thirst with ale. Only the sick and the old, as well as guests who are tired after a long journey, should be given more appetising food.

After giving thanks for the meal, the monks should go back to the chapel for silent meditation, striving not to disturb the tranquility by yawning, sneezing or spitting. Then they should go quietly back to their cells to sleep.

The monks should always be honest with their abbot, sharing their deepest thoughts and feelings with him. All things should be held in common so no book or any other object should be called "mine" or "yours." The monks should wear only simple cloth, made mainly of animal hide.

❖ ❖ ❖

When a person, desiring this holy manner of life, asks to join the community, he must remain for ten days at the door of the monastery, as if he had been rejected; and the monks should be hostile and abusive to him. If he withstands such treatment, keeping his patience until the tenth day, the monk who is doorkeeper should welcome him inside the monastery. Then he must work alongside the monks for many months, obeying the abbot's commands, until the natural stubbornness in his heart has been broken. Finally, according to the abbot's judgement, he should be invited to join the community. On becoming a member, he should renounce any wealth he possesses, giving none to the community, but passing everything to the poor. Thus he comes to the monastery naked, like a man escaping from a shipwreck. In this way all monks will remain equal, with none able to use wealth to raise him above his brethren or avoid the daily toil.

◆ ◆ ◆

◆

SCRIBES AND SCHOLARS

Every monastery had its scribes who copied the Scriptures, and every monk was expected to read and reflect on them with great care. Yet the Celts were never renowned for their scholarship, preferring to express their faith in stories and poetry, rather than theological tracts. And the following verses show us gentle, self-mocking humour at their own intellectual efforts.

◆PRAYER FOR CONCENTRATION◆

God help my thoughts! They stray from me, setting off on the wildest journeys.

When I am in church, they run off like naughty children, quarrelling, making trouble.

◆ ◆ ◆

◆

When I read the Bible, they fly to a distant city, filled with beautiful women.

My thoughts can cross an ocean with a single leap; they can fly from earth to heaven, and back again, in a single second.

They come to me for a fleeting moment, and then away they flee.

No chains, no locks can hold them back; no threats of punishment can restrain them, no hiss of a lash can frighten them.

They slip from my grasp like tails of eels; they swoop hither and thither like swallows in flight.

Dear, chaste Christ, who can see into every heart and read every mind, take hold of my thoughts. Bring my thoughts back to me, and clasp me to yourself.

◆THE SCHOLAR AND HIS CAT◆

I and my white cat each has his special work: his mind is on hunting, while mine is on the pursuit of truth.

To me, better than any worldly thing, is to sit reading, penetrating the mysteries of creation. My cat does not envy me, but prefers his own sport.

We are never bored at home, for we each have endless enjoyment in our own activities, exercising our skills to the utmost.

Sometimes, after a desperate struggle, he catches a mouse in his mouth; as for me, I may catch some difficult law, hard to comprehend, in my mind.

He points his clear bright eye against the wall from which the mice emerge; I point my eye, feeble as it is, against the great wall of knowledge, from which truth emerges.

He enjoys darting around, striving to stick his claw into a mouse; I am happy striving to grasp some complex idea.

So long as we live in this way, neither disturbs the other; each of us loves his work, enjoying it all alone.

◆ ◆ ◆

◆

The task which he performs is the one for which he was created; and I am competent at my task, bringing darkness to light.

✦THE SCRIBE✦

My hand is weary from writing; my sharp quill is not steady; as its tender tip spits its dark, blue stream, the words which are formed on the page are jagged and uncertain.

O Lord, may it be your wisdom, not my folly, which passes through my arm and hand; may your words take shape upon the page. For when I am truly faithful to your dictation, my hand is firm and strong.

Let me never write words that are callous or profane; let your priceless jewels shine upon these pages.

✦THE WEEPING SCHOLAR✦

I read and write. I worship my God every day and every night.

I study the Scriptures, puzzling over their meaning. I write books for the guidance of others.

I eat little, and sleep little. When I eat I continue praying, and when I sleep my snores are songs of praise.

Yet I weep for my sins, because I cannot forget them. O Mary, O Christ, have mercy on this wretched soul.

PRAYERS THROUGH THE DAY

The Celts—like the modern British—were never regular churchgoers, preferring to offer prayers in the course of their daily lives. There are thus numerous traditional prayers, to be offered through the day. Included here is an Evening Hymn traditionally ascribed to Patrick.

•THE RISING•

Let us go forth,
In the goodness of our merciful Father,
In the gentleness of our brother Jesus,
In the radiance of his Holy Spirit,
In the faith of the apostles,
In the joyful praise of the angels,
In the holiness of the saints,
In the courage of martyrs.

◆ ◆ ◆

◆

Let us go forth
In the wisdom of our all-seeing Father,
In the patience of our all-loving brother,
In the truth of the all-knowing Spirit,
In the learning of the apostles,
In the gracious guidance of the angels,
In the patience of the saints,
In the self-control of the martyrs.

Such is the path for all servants of Christ,
The path from death to eternal life.

◆ MORNING PRAYER ◆

The will of God be done by us;
The law of God be kept by us;
Our evil will controlled by us;
Our sharp tongue checked by us;
Quick forgiveness offered by us;
Speedy repentance made by us;
Temptation sternly shunned by us;
Blessed death welcomed by us;
Angels' music heard by us;
God's highest praises sung by us.

◆   ◆   ◆

◆

• KINDLING THE FIRE •

This morning, as I kindle the fire upon my hearth, I pray that the flame of God's love may burn in my heart, and the hearts of all I meet today.

I pray that no envy and malice, no hatred or fear, may smother the flame.

I pray that indifference and apathy, contempt and pride, may not pour like cold water on the fire.

Instead, may the spark of God's love light the love in my heart, that it may burn brightly through the day.

And may I warm those that are lonely, whose hearts are cold and lifeless, so that all may know the comfort of God's love.

• GRACE BEFORE FOOD •

Dear Lord, bless this food for our use, and us for your service.

May the food restore our strength, giving new energy to tired limbs, new thought to weary minds.

May the wine restore our souls, giving new vision to dry spirits, new warmth to cold hearts.

And once refreshed, we offer again our minds and bodies, our hearts and spirits, to proclaim your glory.

•PATRICK'S EVENING HYMN•

O Christ, Son of the living God,
May your holy angels guard our sleep.
May they watch us as we rest
And hover around our beds.

Let them reveal to us in our dreams
Visions of your glorious truth,
O High Prince of the universe,
O High Priest of the mysteries.

May no dreams disturb our rest
And no nightmares darken our dreams.

◆　◆　◆

◆

May no fears or worries delay
Our willing, prompt repose.

May the virtue of our daily work
Hallow our nightly prayers.
May our sleep be deep and soft,
So our work be fresh and hard.

◆COVERING THE FIRE◆

Lord, preserve the fire, as Christ preserves us all.

Lord, may its warmth remain in our midst, as Christ is always among us.

Lord, may it rise to life in the morning, as we shall rise with Christ to eternal life.

◆A NIGHT PRAYER◆

May we do the will of God, with the death of Christ, and rise in the light of heaven.

May we rest safely this night, sleep in perfect peace, and rise with the morning light.

May the Father watch over our beds, Christ fill our dreams, and the angels guard our souls.

◆   ◆   ◆

◆

PRAYERS FOR PROTECTION

The Celts believed that their saints protected them from danger, and two of their most famous prayers for protection are ascribed to Patrick and Brigid respectively.

•ST. PATRICK'S BREASTPLATE•

I gird myself today with the might of
   heaven:
The rays of the sun,
The beams of the moon,
The glory of fire,
The speed of wind,
The depth of sea,
The stability of earth,
The hardness of rock.

I gird myself today with the power of
   God:
God's strength to comfort me,
God's might to uphold me,
God's wisdom to guide me,
God's eye to look before me,
God's ear to hear me,
God's word to speak for me,
God's hand to lead me,
God's way to lie before me,
God's shield to protect me,
God's angels to save me
From the snares of the devil,
From temptations to sin,
From all who wish me ill,
Both far and near,
Alone and with others.

May Christ guard me today
From poison and fire,
From drowning and wounding,
So my mission may bear
Fruit in abundance.
Christ behind and before me,

Christ beneath and above me,
Christ with me and in me,
Christ around and about me,
Christ on my left and my right,
Christ when I rise in the morning,
Christ when I lie down at night,
Christ in each heart that thinks of me,
Christ in each mouth that speaks of me,
Christ in each eye that sees me,
Christ in each ear that hears me.

I arise today
Through the power of the Trinity,
Through faith in the threeness,
Through trust in the oneness,
Of the Maker of earth,
And the Maker of heaven.

◆BRIGID'S BLESSING◆

Every day I pray to St. Brigid that . . .

No fire, no flame shall burn me;
No lake, no sea shall drown me;
No sword, no spear shall wound me;
No king, no chief insult me.

◆ ◆ ◆

◆

All the birds shall sing for me;
All the cattle low for me;
All the insects buzz for me;
God's angels shall protect me.

•PRAYER FOR A LONG LIFE•

Wait for me, King of Heaven, until I am pure, fit to live in your house.

Wait for me, Mary's Son, until I am old, wise from the passing of years.

When a young boy is carried off before his years of playing are over, no one knows what greatness he has missed; only in adulthood comes the full bloom of our gifts.

A calf should not be killed before it is full-grown, nor a pig slaughtered when it is still sucking at the sow's breast.

A bough should not be cut until it has flowered, nor a field harvested until the grain is full.

The sun should not set at midday, nor rise at midnight.

Keep my soul here on earth, for it is like soft, unformed clay, not ready to be received by you.

Yet even if you cut me off in my youth, I shall not complain, but continue to worship you.

◆DANGER OF DEATH◆

When I go out alone on the mountain, O King of roads, may my journey be safe. Death is no nearer to me on the mountain peak, than if I were guarded by three thousand men.

Even if I had three thousand young men with armour of the thickest hide, when the call of death comes there is no fortress that could hold out against it.

Even if I had no protection whatever, there is no snare that could trap me if death was not calling.

If someone tries to ambush me and steal my goods, he will not succeed unless the Lord allows it.

No mere human being can shorten my life, unless it is shortened by the King who shaped the earth and sends the seasons.

I ignore all omens that people say bring ill-luck, because God alone determines our fortunes and misfortunes.

The warrior whose clean white flesh is cut open with a sword need have no greater fear of death than a man who cowers at home.

Everyone has only one day of real danger, and that is the day on which he dies.

So I have no fear of earthly dangers; I fear God alone—and him do I trust.

PRAYERS OF LIFE AND DEATH

The passing of time, and the brevity of human life, are constant themes of Celtic poetry. But death is not to be feared, but rather embraced as part of God's natural order.

◆TIME◆

Take no oath by the earth that you stand on. You walk on it only for a while, but soon you shall be buried within it.

Pay no heed to the world you live in. You are dazzled by its pomp and pleasure, but soon you shall be carried from it.

Time is like the ebbing tide on the beach. You cannot see it move by staring at it, but soon it has run away from sight.

◆   ◆   ◆

◆

•THE TREE OF LIFE•

O King of the Tree of Life,
The blossoms on the branches are your
  people,
The singing birds are your angels,
The whispering breeze is your Spirit.

O King of the Tree of Life,
May the blossoms bring forth the
  sweetest fruit,
May the birds sing out the highest praise,
May your Spirit cover all with his gentle
  breath.

•YOUTH AND AGE•

Once my hair was shining yellow, falling in
long ringlets round my brow; now it is grey
and sparse, all lustre gone.

Once as I walked along the lane girls' heads
would turn to look at me; now no woman
looks my way, no heart races as I approach.

Once my body was filled with desire, and
I had energy to satisfy my every want;

now desire has grown dim, I have no energy to satisfy even the few desires that remain.

Yet I would prefer chilly age to hot youth; I would rather know that God is near, than have no thought of him in my head.

I have had my day on earth; now I look to eternity in heaven.

◆ FINAL REFLECTIONS ◆

I give you thanks, my King, for the care you have lavished upon me.

I have for six months been lying on my bed, my body racked by disease; I am a prisoner, held in chains by my illness.

My strength is gone, from my head to my feet I can barely move; my weakness is like fetters holding me down.

I am like a blind man unable to see the world around me; for six months I have seen only the walls of my hut.

◆   ◆   ◆

◆

You have nailed me to my cross; this sickness is my crucifixion.

And so I give you thanks, my King, for bringing me joyfully to judgement.

Tomorrow I shall die, and see you face to face; tomorrow your lash on my body shall cease, and I shall be at peace.

If now my body is shrouded by clouds of darkness, my soul basks in warm light; if now my eyes are filled with bitter tears, my soul can taste the sweetest honey.

I am like a mouse, caught in a trap and shaken in the claws of a cat; tomorrow I shall be as free as the wind.

My present pains are as nothing compared to the enormity of my sin; your mercy is infinite and eternal.

◆DYING DAY◆

When your eyes are closing and your mouth opening, may God bring you comfort on that day.

◆ ◆ ◆

◆

When your senses are fading and your limbs growing cold, may God save your soul on that day.

Pray to Michael and to all the angels, pray to Mary and to all the saints, that God will pour out his mercy on that day.

Pray that the Virgin will reach out and embrace you, that Michael will reach down and lift you up, on the day of your death.

◆REMEMBER YOUR END◆

Remember, O friend, your end.

Now you are strong and fit, filled with ambition, boasting of your achievements; but all your success is a mere passing shadow.

Remember you are made of clay, and to clay you will return.

Now you are healthy and handsome, filled with energy, proud of your work; but all your joys are mere passing shadows.

Remember your life is the breath of God, which at death will depart.

Now your life on earth is solid and stable; but soon it will dissolve, your body crumbling to dust.

Remember, O friend, your end.

SONGS TO JESUS

Celtic literature contains a large number of songs celebrating the life of Jesus. Their sources are not just the canonical gospels, but also the apocryphal gospels such as that ascribed to St. Thomas—which is further evidence of Celtic links with the church in Egypt, where these gospels were especially popular.

◆ PREGNANCY ◆

The Master of the Angels descended on Mary, lighting a flame of pure love within her womb.

She was not a queen nor a princess; she was not rich nor famous.

She sought no glory for herself; she desired only to obey God's will.

◆   ◆   ◆

◆

Yet her womb became the palace of the highest King; her belly carried the most glorious Prince.

She received the spark of glory; she brought the full light of God's love into the world.

◆ BIRTH ◆

Greetings, Holy Child; welcome, Word of God.

Now you sleep in a manger, in a stable poor and cold; but for us you are the highest King, making our hearts into your palace.

Now you have a human mother, to carry you into the world; but for us you are the Son of the high God, sent to carry us to heaven.

Mary is young, and Joseph hardly grown; but you were made when time began, and shall live to all eternity.

◆ INFANCY ◆

Mary nursed you in her little hut; you grew up in the humblest hovel.

◆   ◆   ◆

◆

You crawled on a cold earth floor; you warmed yourself by a meagre fire.

She clasped you to her bosom when you cried; she sang sweet lullabies as your eyelids closed in sleep.

Did she know who you were? Could she foresee your life and death, your rising and ascending?

To her you were more precious than gold, more beautiful than the finest jewel.

◆MARY'S VISION◆

"Are you asleep, Mother?"

"No, I am awake, dear son."

"Why are you awake, Mother?"

"Because I am distressed by a vision of you."

"What is that vision, Mother?"

"It is a slim dark man, on a black horse, with a long sharp lance in his left hand. He pierces your right side, and blood gushes out."

"Where does the blood fall, Mother?"

"Into my heart, and into the hearts of all that love you."

◆ BOYHOOD ◆

When he was barely five years old, Jesus blessed twelve small pools; and he built a wall of clay around them.

Then he moulded twelve small birds out of clay, and placed them by the pools.

All this he did on the Sabbath day.

A Jewish elder, seeing what Jesus was doing, took Joseph by the hand: "Punish your son, Joseph, for he is breaking the Sabbath."

Jesus clapped his hands and cried out, in a clear pure voice: "Go home, little birds, to the One who made you."

The clay birds came to life, and flew upwards to heaven, singing the praises of God.

◆　◆　◆

◆

◆EDUCATION◆

The wise Zacharias said: "This boy is wonderful. He would be even more wonderful if he were educated."

So Zacharias took Jesus to his school, to teach him how to read.

But whenever Zacharias asked Jesus a question, Jesus did not answer, remaining silent. Zacharias got angry, and hit Jesus on the head with a stick.

At last Jesus spoke, quoting an ancient proverb: "An anvil that is struck teaches the one who strikes it."

Zacharias replied: "Go away and teach yourself—and then come back to tell me what you have learnt."

◆MINISTRY◆

Fair Jesus, you guide your straying sheep along lush and fragrant valleys, where the grass is rich and deep.

You guard them from the attacks of wolves, and from the bites of snakes.

You heal their diseases, and teach them always to walk in the ways of God.

When we stray, lead us back; when temptation besets us, give us strength; when our souls are sick, pour upon us your love.

◆HEALING◆

Behold, Jesus, the woman with the swollen breasts; the tumour on her chest is as large and red as a rose.

Behold, Jesus, the man whose eyes are blind; the eyeballs are covered with a thick shell, through which no light can pass.

Behold, Jesus, the woman bleeding; blood oozes from her body like bitter wine, staining the ground on which she walks.

Behold, Jesus, the man whose legs are wasted; they are like two spindly sticks, which crack when he crawls.

◆ ◆ ◆

◆

Pluck the rose, dissolve the shells, staunch the flow, strengthen the sticks, that all may reflect your glory.

◆ENEMIES◆

When Christ's enemies were looking for him, chasing him through villages and over hills, they met a butterfly and a beetle.

They asked these two insects: "Have you seen the man they call the Christ?"

"Yes," said the butterfly, without guile. "He has just passed this way, and you shall find him travelling east."

"Yes," said the beetle, knowing their hearts were as black as his skin. "He passed this way yesterday, and was travelling towards the west."

Christ's enemies did not know whom to believe, or whether both were lying. So they trod on both the butterfly and the beetle, and then divided, some going east and some west.

◆ ◆ ◆

◆

But they did not catch the Christ; he only let himself be captured when the time was ripe.

◆DEATH◆

I adore the suffering King who feels my suffering; I love the sorrowing Lord who knows my sorrow.

At his death no fire came upon his captors to burn them, no great flood rose to sweep them away, the earth did not open to swallow them up, the sky did not fall to crush them.

No fierce birds came to attack Pilate, no wild beast mauled the priests and scribes, no snake rose up to bite those who whipped Jesus.

He allowed them to accuse him falsely, without opening his mouth; he let them drag him to the cross with no words of reproof; he watched quietly as they drove nails into his hands and feet.

He who created the universe, he who preserves the universe, he whom the sun and

◆   ◆   ◆

◆

moon obey, he who rules the stars, forsook his mighty power.

So he suffered with us who suffer much; he sorrowed with us who feel much sorrow.

◆ BURIAL ◆

O blessed Lord, your body is cold as the stone around you, your skin as white as the shroud that covers you.

O blessed Lord, you are all alone in the tomb, your friends too frightened to come near you.

O blessed Lord, my heart is cold, my soul is white with fear; I feel lonely, I have no friends at my side.

I wait for your glory, when the bright sun of God's love will warm all mankind, and everyone will be at peace with his neighbour.

◆ RESURRECTION ◆

I rise with you, dear Jesus, and you rise with me.

◆ ◆ ◆

As the oil of gladness pours upon you, it trickles onto me.

As the fire of love burns within you, it warms my heart.

As the breath of eternal life fills your body, I know that I shall live for ever.

As the Word of God comes from your lips, your name is written forever on my forehead.

As you reach out to bless mankind, I feel your embrace drawing me close.

I rise with you, dear Jesus, and you rise with me.

GOD AND THE SOUL

Compared with other Christian traditions, Celtic spirituality contains few direct meditations on God and the soul's relationship with him. Yet, as one would expect, such meditations as exist are filled with images of nature. The first and second poems here are taken from The Black Book of Camarthan, an ancient Welsh work. The final piece is a catechism usually ascribed to Ninian, which again reflects the Celtic respect for nature.

·GOD·

I am the wind that breathes upon the sea,
I am the wave on the ocean,
I am the murmur of leaves rustling,
I am the rays of the sun,

I am the beam of the moon and stars,
I am the power of trees growing,
I am the bud breaking into blossom,
I am the movement of the salmon
   swimming,
I am the courage of the wild boar
   fighting,
I am the speed of the stag running,
I am the strength of the ox pulling the
   plough,
I am the size of the mighty oak tree,
And I am the thoughts of all people
Who praise my beauty and grace.

•THE SOUL•

I am a flame of fire, blazing with passionate
love;

I am a spark of light, illuminating the deepest
truth;

I am a rough ocean, heaving with righteous
anger;

I am a calm lake, comforting the troubled
breast;

I am a wild storm, raging at human sins;

I am a gentle breeze, blowing hope in the saddened heart;

I am dry dust, choking worldly ambition;

I am wet earth, bearing rich fruits of grace.

◆GOD'S WILL◆

Anyone who rejects God's will
Is like a leaking ship on a stormy sea,
Is like an eagle caught in a trap,
Is like an apple tree which never
   blossoms.

Anyone who obeys God's will
Is like the golden rays of the summer sun,
Is like a silver chalice overflowing with
   wine,
Is like a beautiful bride ready for love.

◆A MILLION MIRACLES◆

O Son of God, perform a miracle for me: change my heart. You, whose crimson blood redeems mankind, whiten my heart.

◆ ◆ ◆

◆

It is you who makes the sun bright and the ice sparkle; you who makes the rivers flow and the salmon leap.

Your skilled hand makes the nut tree blossom, and the corn turn golden; your Spirit composes the songs of the birds and the buzz of the bees.

Your creation is a million wondrous miracles, beautiful to behold. I ask of you just one more miracle: beautify my soul.

◆LORD OF MY HEART◆

Lord of my heart, give me vision to inspire me, that, working or resting, I may always think of you.

Lord of my heart, give me light to guide me, that, at home or abroad, I may always walk in your way.

Lord of my heart, give me wisdom to direct me, that, thinking or acting, I may always discern right from wrong.

◆ ◆ ◆

◆

Lord of my heart, give me courage to strengthen me, that, amongst friends or enemies, I may always proclaim your justice.

Lord of my heart, give me trust to console me, that, hungry or well-fed, I may always rely on your mercy.

Lord of my heart, save me from empty praise, that I may always boast of you.

Lord of my heart, save me from worldly wealth, that I may always look to the riches of heaven.

Lord of my heart, save me from military prowess, that I may always seek your protection.

Lord of my heart, save me from vain knowledge, that I may always study your Word.

Lord of my heart, save me from unnatural pleasures, that I may always find joy in your wonderful creation.

Heart of my own heart, whatever may befall me, rule over my thoughts and feelings, my words and actions.

• I LIE DOWN WITH GOD •

I lie down with God; may God lie down with me.

May the right hand of God be under my head, and the two hands of Mary embrace me.

May the angels of God support me, from the top of my head to the soles of my feet.

I shall never lie down with evil; may evil never lie down with me.

Mary, mother of Jesus, and Elizabeth, mother of John, nurse me when I fall sick, and restore me to health.

Jesus, nailed to the cross, and John, beheaded by Herod, be close to me when I die, and carry me to heaven.

• CONFESSION •

Jesus, forgive my sins.

Forgive the sins that I can remember, and also the sins I have forgotten.

Forgive the wrong actions I have committed, and the right actions I have omitted.

Forgive the times I have been weak in the face of temptation, and those when I have been stubborn in the face of correction.

Forgive the times I have been proud of my own achievements, and those when I have failed to boast of your works.

Forgive the harsh judgements I have made of others, and the leniency I have shown to myself.

Forgive the lies I have told to others, and the truths I have avoided.

Forgive me the pain I have caused others, and the indulgence I have shown to myself.

Jesus have pity on me, and make me whole.

◆ THE SOUL'S DESIRE ◆

My soul's desire is to see the face of God, and to rest in his house.

◆   ◆   ◆

◆

My soul's desire is to study the Scriptures, and to learn the ways of God.

My soul's desire is to be freed from all fear and sadness, and to share Christ's risen life.

My soul's desire is to imitate my King, and to sing his praises always.

My soul's desire is to enter the gates of heaven, and to gaze upon the light that shines forever.

Dear Lord, you alone know what my soul truly desires, and you alone can satisfy those desires.

◆NINIAN'S CATECHISM◆

QUESTION: What is best in this world?

ANSWER: To do the will of our Maker.

QUESTION: What is his will?

ANSWER: That we should live according to the laws of his creation.

QUESTION: How do we know those laws?

ANSWER: By study—studying the Scriptures with devotion.

◆　◆　◆

◆

QUESTION: What tool has our Maker provided for this study?

ANSWER: The intellect, which can probe everything.

QUESTION: And what is the fruit of study?

ANSWER: To perceive the eternal Word of God reflected in every plant and insect, every bird and animal, and every man and woman.

RICHES AND POVERTY

Averse to theological or mystical speculation, the Celts were especially attracted to the practical, moral teachings of Christ. They saw him as the champion of the poor and downtrodden, and the scourge of the wealthy and powerful. Included here are two short dramas depicting rich people encountering death—a favourite literary device for making moral points.

◆ A RICH MAN DISPUTES WITH DEATH ◆

RICH MAN: I have never done anything that I thought deserved much blame, let alone eternal punishment. I have never committed a sin like murder or treachery, theft or arson.

I have done much that deserves praise, much to merit eternal reward. I have welcomed travelers into my home, and given food to the hungry.

Surely God could not condemn such a man as me.

DEATH: I have no doubt that everything you say is true. I know that you neither kill nor steal, and that you help the needy.

Yet when you were young you boasted of your riches, imagining yourself superior because of your ability to gain wealth. And now you boast of your virtue, imagining yourself superior because of your capacity to give to others.

RICH MAN: You are mistaken. I am gentle and meek, never speaking any proud words about my wealth and my virtue.

You do me injustice. I am humble and contrite, regularly confessing my sins before God.

DEATH: I have no doubt that everything you say is true. I know that you neither boast nor flaunt your wealth, and you say prayers of confession.

But a man can speak without words, can boast without talking of his wealth and virtue. A proud heart is the mother of boastful actions; and actions speak louder than words.

RICH MAN: So I am to be condemned for words I have not said, for sins I have not committed.

How then can a man be saved? How then can I gain eternal life?

DEATH: You can be saved by tears which

dissolve your pride. You can gain eternal life by forgetting your wealth and virtue, remembering only the Creator of all wealth, the source of all virtue.

◆ A QUEEN MEETS DEATH ◆

DEATH: Most beautiful Queen, you must say farewell to all your friends before dusk today. Now your health and wealth, your life itself, are in my power; tonight I shall carry you away.

QUEEN: How dare you break into my room! Who are you, with your dark face and furrowed brow?

DEATH: I am the one to whom all people alive must one day become slaves. Now you, ravishing Queen, are my slave. Now I shall sever you from the world, and carry you into God's presence.

◆ ◆ ◆

◆

QUEEN: Is that the reason that I must forsake my lands and my wealth, leave my fine castle filled with gold and jewels, abandon my flocks of white sheep and herds of sleek cattle? Do you ask me to come with you, without even a coin in my hand?

DEATH: I do not ask, I order. In this world men asked favours of you, and you have given orders. Now it is I who give orders, and I grant no favours.

QUEEN: What shall I do with my fine horses, with my barns full of corn? I refuse to come with you; I shall order my bravest soldiers to drive you from my castle, never to return.

DEATH: My task, dear Queen, is to travel from village to village, from house to house, taking with me whomever God orders. Queens and prostitutes, princes and peasants, are all alike to me; and no soldier's sword can cut me down.

QUEEN: Could you not delay your dreadful deed? Could you not wait until my daughter has married one of the rich handsome men who court her? Could you not take my hand only, that you may enjoy its blessing?

DEATH: Your daughter shall marry whomever she is destined to marry. And your hand shall remain firmly attached to your body, which tomorrow shall inhabit a cold, stone tomb.

QUEEN: Many is the poor man that walks past my castle who is hungry and cold, sick and miserable. Take such a man who has no hope in this world, and leave me who rejoices in the world.

DEATH: Now you tell me the reason why I must take you. If you had shared

your joy with the poor who pass
your gate, then you could stay.

QUEEN: Now I feel my head swelling, my
heart burning, my belly aching, my
breast thumping. O Death, take
from me this pain, and let me die in
peace.

DEATH: In your time you have seen many
suffer in terrible pain, you have
watched many die in agony, but you
have not even offered wine to ease
their misery. Now your candle flick-
ers, now you must make yourself
ready to give your account.

QUEEN: Give me some relief from this disease.
If you would help me now, I would
call you a gentleman, a man of honour. If you reject my plea, you are
no better than the meanest peasant.

DEATH: You condemn yourself with your
own mouth. You regard the poor

◆   ◆   ◆

◆

with contempt, while not once looking to God for help. I implore you to beg his mercy.

QUEEN: I am too proud to beg, and too weak to change. If I condemn myself, I stand condemned.

• THE RICH MAN'S SOUL •

Let me take you inside the soul of a rich man without love, and a wealthy man without friends.

The darkest night, with neither moon nor stars, is like the brightest day compared with the darkness of this soul.

The coldest winter, with thick snow and hard ice, is like the warmest summer compared with the coldness of this soul.

The bleakest mountain, bare and swept by gales, is like the lushest meadow compared with the bleakness of this soul.

You would rather have your body hacked in pieces than present such a soul as this; you would rather be boiled or burned alive than suffer such inward torment.

✦THE RICH MAN'S FRIENDS✦

Amongst the sleek and wealthy, the poor are regarded as fools.

Once I was wealthy, and flocks of friends thronged my door; I grew poor, and none came near.

In summer people wanted to walk in my shadow; now as I pass in my coarse tunic they avoid me.

The person they saw when I was rich was not me, but my wealth; now they see nobody, pretending I no longer exist.

If I were rich again, their eyes would brighten as they saw me, and their arms reach out to embrace me; now they can watch me collapse without lifting a hand to help me.

The world jibes at me because my barns are bare and my hut empty; the proud peer down their noses at me, the rich curl their lips.

✦ ✦ ✦

✦

O Lord, let everyone know both wealth and poverty in their lives; then all will be happy to share what they have.

Remember the poor when you look out on fields you own, on your plump cows grazing.

Remember the poor when you look into your barn, at the abundance of your harvest.

Remember the poor when the wind howls and the rain falls, as you sit warm and dry in your house.

Remember the poor when you eat fine meat and drink fine ale, at your fine carved table.

The cows have grass to eat, the rabbits have burrows for shelter, the birds have warm nests.

But the poor have no food except what you feed them, no shelter except your house when you welcome them, no warmth except your glowing fire.

THE CELTIC PSALTER

The Celtic Psalter *is the longest religious poem to emerge from early Ireland. It is divided into 150 shorter poems in imitation of the Psalms of David, and it relates the entire biblical story, from the creation to the resurrection. It is traditionally attributed to Oengus the Culdee, an Irish hermit living in the ninth century. The finest parts—and the most Celtic in tone—are from the beginning, which are given here.*

•CREATION OF THE WORLD•

My dear King, my own King, without pride, without sin, you created the whole world, eternal, victorious King.

King above the elements, King above the sun, King beneath the ocean, King of the north and south, the east and west, against you no enemy can prevail.

King of the Mysteries, you existed before the elements, before the sun was set in the sky, before the waters covered the ocean floor; beautiful King, you are without beginning and without end.

King, you created the daylight, and made the darkness; you are not arrogant or boastful, and yet strong and firm.

King, you created the land out of shapeless maps, you carved the mountains and chiselled the valleys, and covered the earth with trees and grass.

King, you stretched out the sky above the earth, a perfect sphere like a perfect apple, and you decorated the sky with stars to shine at night.

King, you pierced the earth with springs from which pure water flows, to form streams and rivers across the land.

◆ ◆ ◆

◆

King, you ordained the eight winds, the four primary winds from north and south, east and west, and the four lesser winds that swirl hither and thither.

You gave each wind its own colour: the north wind is white, bringing snow in winter; the south wind is red, carrying warmth in summer; the west wind is blue, a cooling breeze across the sea; the east wind is yellow, scorching in summer and bitter in winter; and the lesser winds are green, orange, purple and black— the black wind that blows in the darkest nights.

King, you measured each object and each span within the universe: the heights of the mountains and the depths of the oceans; the distance from the sun to the moon, and from star to star.

You ordained the movements of every object: the sun to cross the sky each day, and the moon to rise each night; the clouds to carry rain from the sea, and the rivers to carry water back from the sea.

King, you divided the earth into three zones: the north cold and bitter; the south hot and dry; and the middle zone cool, wet and fertile.

And you created men and women to be your stewards of the earth, always praising you for your boundless love.

◆CREATION OF HEAVEN◆

King, you created heaven according to your delight, a place that is safe and pure, its air filled with the songs of angels.

It is like a strong mighty city, which no enemy can invade, with walls as high as mountains.

It is like an open meadow, in which all can move freely, with people arriving from earth but never leaving.

It is huge, ten times the size of earth, so that every creature ever born can find a place.

◆ ◆ ◆

◆

It is small, no bigger than a village, where all are friends, and none is a stranger.

In the centre is a palace, its walls made of emerald and its gates of amethyst; and on each gate is hung a golden cross.

The roof is ruby, and at each pinnacle stands an eagle covered in gold, its eyes of sapphire.

Inside the palace it is always daylight, and the air cool, neither hot nor cold; and there is a perfect green lawn, with a blue stream running across it.

At the edge of this lawn are trees and shrubs, always in blossom, white, pink and purple, spreading a sweet fragrance everywhere.

Round the lawn walks a King, not dressed in fine robes, but in a simple white tunic, smiling and embracing those he meets.

And people from outside are constantly entering the palace, mingling one with another, and then leaving.

Everyone in heaven is free to come to the palace, and then to take with them its perfect peaceful joy; and in this way the whole of heaven is infused with the joy of the palace.

THE FOUR SEASONS

In a number of collections of Celtic poetry there are similar poems about the seasons of the year. While the particular images vary, they all depict each season as having a human face.

◆SPRING◆

The face of nature laughs in the springtime, her breath fresh and her eyes clearest blue.

Horses gather at the river's edge to drink its fresh clean water; the sparkling waterfall cries with joy as its torrent hits the rocks.

The blackbird's call is wild and free, rejoicing at the new abundance of food; the cuckoo, that lover of warmth, begins its happy chorus.

◆　◆　◆

◆

Sheep and cattle gobble the crisp, juicy grass; the meadows are alight with the colours of flowers in bloom.

The sun glints through the fresh green leaves; the wind rustling through the branches in the harp of nature, playing a song of love.

Men are vigorous and strong, women pretty and gay; the whole world is in love with its Creator.

◆ SUMMER ◆

Nature's face smiles in the summer, her breath sweet, her eyes soft hazel.

The sea is calm, its waves gently licking the sandy beach; the rivers skip quietly down the valleys, speckled salmon leaping in their crystal waters.

Bees struggle to carry in their feet the sticky harvest from the flowers; ants scurry hither and thither to gather food.

It is the season for long journeys, for the days are long; robbers have no darkness to hide their evil deeds, so the lanes are safe.

A cheerful breeze sweeps the tops of the trees, while below the heat settles on the earth; the dogs are too warm to bark, the cats too lazy to hunt.

Men must rest every hour from their sweaty labours, and women work in the shade; people are at peace with their Creator.

·AUTUMN·

Nature's face is lined with care in the autumn, her breath short and her eyes golden-brown.

The rivers are murky and low, and the ponds muddy and slimy; neither people nor animals can find clear water to drink.

The birds are fat with eating the berries of the hedges; they must fill their bellies before the days grow cold and short.

The horses are weary carrying the heavy harvest on their backs; the grass which the sheep and cattle eat is thick and tough.

The leaves turn yellow at the edges, and then become brown and brittle; the winds blow them from their branches.

Men spend every hour in the fields cutting the corn, while the women gather fruits and nuts from the forest; people have no time to remember their Creator.

·WINTER·

The face of nature is solemn in winter, her breath chill, and her eyes pale.

Ducks shiver as they float on icy ponds; the sea heaves, its waves beating against the cliffs.

The birds' song is muffled and sad, as they search for scraps of food; only the ravens are glad, feeding on crimson blood.

The tiny animals are asleep in their holes, with food for the winter; the cattle and sheep huddle for warmth.

The trees are bare, the wind whistling through their branches; the earth is barren and dark, covered with black wet leaves.

The men cut wood for the fire, while the women cook hot, thin soup; people contemplate death, when they shall meet their Creator.

THE ENCOUNTERS
OF MOLING

Moling was a monk at Glendalough some years after Kevin's death. Almost nothing is known about him, apart from his encounters with the devil and an angel.

•THE DEVIL VISITS MOLING•

One day Moling was praying in church when he saw a man coming towards him, dressed in a fine purple robe. The man reached out to embrace Moling, but Moling remained motionless.

"Why do you not welcome me?" the man asked.

"Who are you?" Moling asked in reply.

"I am Christ, the Son of God," the man answered.

"I do not know that," Moling grunted.

"When Christ comes to talk to his servants, he does not wear the fine tunic of a nobleman, but comes in the form of a leper or a beggar."

"So you don't believe me," said the man haughtily. "Then why do you suppose I am here?"

"I suppose that you are the devil, and you have come to tempt me."

Moling then took in his hand the Bible that lay in front of him, and raised it up. The man recoiled in pain, and then fell to his knees.

"Dear saint," begged the man, "I have come here to receive your blessing. I implore you, put your hand on my head and bless me."

"I will not bestow a blessing," retorted Moling. "You do not deserve it. And besides, what good would it do?"

"If I were to bathe in a tub of honey," replied the man, "its sweet odour would stay with me for longer afterwards. Your blessing would be honey to my unclean soul."

"A sweet smell serves only to deceive, if the object itself is dirty and poisonous," said Moling.

❖　❖　❖

❖

"Then," cried the man, "give me your curse."

"A curse is contained in every word you utter, so why should I just add to your curse?"

"Most noble saint," pleaded the man, his voice choking with tears; "Tell me what I must do to become holy. Should I fast, pray, cut my hair, wear rags—what must I do?"

"Only one thing, and one thing alone can save you," said Moling gravely. "Go off into the forest and live entirely alone. Never again try to disturb the peace of God's people. Then in his good time, God will come to visit you, and take you to himself."

The man left Moling, for Moling's command was impossible for him.

•AN ANGEL VISITS MOLING•

One day a young man carrying a harp came to Moling's monastery. All the monks, except Moling himself, were in the refectory eating their supper. The young man asked if he could play for them, and they gladly agreed. After he had finished playing, they invited him to share their meal.

❖   ❖   ❖

As he was eating the young man asked which of them was Moling, whose holiness was so famous. The monks replied that Moling was in church, as this was one of the three days each week when he fasted. After the meal the young man took his harp and walked towards the church. The monks shook their heads, knowing that Moling never allowed himself the pleasure of hearing music.

When the young man entered the church Moling was kneeling in prayer. The young man sat next to the altar and began to play. Moling did not lift his head, but took from his pocket two balls of wax, and stuffed them into his ears.

The young man smiled and continued playing. To Moling's amazement the wax in his ears began to melt; and, try as he might to push it back into his ears, it just dribbled down his neck and under his cassock.

At that moment the young man took a small stone and began scraping it up and down the strings of the harp, so they screeched horribly. Moling found it unbearable, and began to writhe in agony. Then the young man threw the stone away, and played so sweetly that Moling was soothed; and, as the man's fingers moved across the strings, Moling felt greater joy than he had ever known before.

At the end Moling asked: "Are you a devil sent to tempt me, or an angel sent to bless me?"

"You must make your own judgement," the young man replied. "When I scraped my harp with a stone, it made the noise of the devil. And when I played it with my fingers it made the sound of an angel. Music, like food and drink, can be an agent of evil, or a source of goodness."

The young man then got up and left. From that moment Moling welcomed all musicians to play at the monastery. And he gave up fasting, except on those days when everyone must fast. His brethren could not help noticing that from that moment onwards he became more gentle and kind, and even acquired a sense of humour.

THE VISION OF SETH

*In this ancient Cornish drama Seth, a young man,
visits the gate of Paradise, and is granted a vision
which is remarkably similar to that contained in* The
Celtic Psalter.

ANGEL: Seth, what is your purpose? Why do
        you make this long journey?

SETH: Angel, I will tell you. My father is
        old and weary, and no longer wishes
        to live. Through me he prays that
        you will give the oil of mercy, to
        prepare him for the last day.

ANGEL: Put your head inside the gate, and

look in every direction. Examine it well, and do not be fearful.

SETH: I will gladly look. It is a great honour to see what is there, and then go back to tell what I see to my father.

(Seth now looks through the gate)

SETH: I see a most beautiful field. The tongue of man could never describe its wonders. There are trees laden with succulent fruit, and the grass is speckled with flowers of every colour. There are minstrels singing the sweetest melodies. There is a fountain as bright as silver, with four springs of water flowing from it. In the middle of the field there is a high tree with countless branches stretching out like great arms. But all the branches are bare, without a single leaf, and there is no bark on the trunk. And at the bottom I can see its roots descending into the darkness of hell.

ANGEL: Look again. Mark everything you see. Can you see something more?

SETH: I see a serpent in the tree, a most terrifying ugly creature.

ANGEL: Look again. Mark everything you see. Can you see anything more?

SETH: High up in the branches of the tree I see a tiny child, newly born. He is wrapped in pure white swaddling clothes.

ANGEL: That tiny child, dressed in swaddling clothes, will redeem your father—redeem him both in body and in soul—and redeem your mother too. He is the oil of mercy, to prepare your father and mother for the last day.

SETH: Blessed be that child. Now I am satisfied, for I know the truth.

❖　❖　❖

❖

ANGEL: I shall give you an apple from that great tree. When you get home, cut it into two halves; then cut one half into two quarters, so that you have three pieces, one large and two small. Plant them on the hill near your house, the large piece in the middle. They will grow into three trees, the middle one taller than the others. And they shall each have three branches, one pointing upwards, and the others reaching to either side. Whenever you look towards that hill, it will remind you of the vision you have received this day in Paradise.

GNOMIC POEMS

A popular Welsh literary form was the "gnome": a maxim, preceded by apparently unrelated images. They have something of the quality of the "koan" in Zen Buddhism.

◆ RED IS . . . ◆

Red is the cock's comb, and loud his voice. God praises man when man praises God.

Swift are the streams on the side of the mountain, and sparkling their waters. The unfaithful man envies the peace of the faithful.

Quarrelsome are the geese in the farmyard, and fearsome their wings. The generous man feels richer than the miser.

◆ ◆ ◆

◆

Wet are the furrows in winter, and heavy the ploughing. The grieving heart finds comfort only in grief.

White are the wings of a dove, and plump its body. The greedy man feeds his greed each time he eats.

Joyful are the pigs when food is brought, and eager their eating. The man who uses his talents to the full will be fully satisfied.

◆DELIGHTFUL ARE . . . ◆

Delightful are the tops of ash trees; they grow tall at the head of the valley. A heart filled with desire brings only sadness.

Delightful are the tops of willow trees; the wind whistles through their stately branches. Instinct is stronger than morality.

Delightful are the tops of gorse bushes; their blossom reflects the brightness of the sun. None can know the truth except God.

Delightful are the tops of clover plants; their blossom reflects the darkness of the night. A jealous heart grows weary with anxiety.

Delightful are the tops of oak trees; they provide shade for lovers to meet. The colour of the cheek cannot disguise the feelings of the heart.

Delightful are the tops of apple trees; their flowers turn into sweetest fruit. Those who are too contented grow lazy and sleepy.

Delightful are the tops of holly bushes; their berries glow red in the winter darkness. The man who sees what he loves knows true happiness.

Delightful are the tops of bracken; the leaves give protection to wild animals. Prayer for one who is not loved will have no effect.

◆THE MONTHS OF THE YEAR◆

The month of January, the valley is
foggy.

The wandering minstrel is cold and
weary.

The cow is lean, the hum of the bee
seldom heard.

The udder of the cow is dry, the larder
empty of meat.

The horse is thin, the song of the bird is
silent.

The dawn is late, the dusk early.

"The best candle for man is common-
sense."

The month of February, a feast is rare.

The spade and the wheel are hard at
work.

The ox has no voice to complain.

The evenings grow longer, the mornings
earlier.

The sun grows brighter, but the clouds
are darker.

A rainbow is seen after storms.

"The greatest pleasure is friendship."

The month of March, great is the pride
of the birds.

The wind is bitter blowing over the
   ploughed field.
The crops are short while the days grow
   longer.
Every creature knows its enemy.
Every bird knows its mate.
Every plant springs out of the earth.
"The bold man succeeds, while the
   reckless man fails."

The month of April, the tops of the hills
   are misty.
The oxen pull ploughs across the bare
   land.
The hares are playing in the sunshine of
   spring.
The deer leap after a hungry winter.
People travel to relatives long unvisited.
People laugh at simple humour.
People smile at wicked children's tricks.
"Dignity is a virtue, but arrogance a vice."

The month of May, the grass grows
   green and long.
In every ditch lovers meet.

Even old men feel light of heart.
The leaves on the trees are thick and
strong.
The cuckoo and the hound shout for joy.
The wool on the sheep is thick and
warm.
Even old cows look for a bull.
"Forgiveness is easy where love abounds."

The month of June, beautiful are the
fields.
The sea is smooth, the water sparkling in
the sunlight.
The beaches are golden, the sand soft
and warm.
The day is long, the morning bright.
The peat bogs are firm for sheep to graze.
The women are pretty and playful.
"The man who seeks power will die in
weakness."

The month of July, the heat clings to the
skin.
The hay ricks are smokey, the hay
turning golden-grey.

The fields are dusty, dust hangs in the
air.
The men sweat as they weed the crops.
The old women pant as they churn the
butter.
The young girls hide, and sleep the day
away.
"While men only talk, God discerns and
judges."

The month of August, the beaches now
covered with foam.
The bees are merry, their hives are full.
The sickle swings on ripened corn.
The straw ricks erupt across the fields.
The men toil, ignoring even dusk.
The women pray that the harvest may be
full.
"Those who neither work nor pray shall
starve."

The month of September, the season of
ripening fruit.
The apples are hard, the pears are soft.
The plums are dark, the berries bright.

The eye of God is on the poor.
The fruit is piled high at every door.
The ponds are dry, but stomachs full.
"Though men must rest, God never
   sleeps."

The month of October, the fields again
   are bare.
The axle of the wagon is worn from
   carrying corn.
The wind is swift, attacking yellow
   leaves.
The leaves fall, forming a soft brown floor.
The birds are fat, the fish sleek.
Yet the milk of the cow turns thin and
   pale.
"Faith is better than fasting, and love
   crowns both."

The month of November, the swine are
   plump.
The trees are now half bare, the leaves
   half fallen.
The brown floor turns black and sodden.
The days grow shorter, the nights longer.

The rain grows colder, the sunshine
   paler.
The full barn soon starts to empty.
"The wealth of heaven lasts forever."

The month of December, the time of
   darkest days.
The land is heavy, the sun weary.
The trees are bare, the people warmly
   wrapped.
The bee and the nightingale are silent.
Mud clings to boots, so walking is slow.
Only the cock sings a merry song.
"In God there is no night and day."

TRIADS

The triad originated as a simple mnemonic: before the Irish learnt to read and write, laws and instructions were frequently memorised in this form. Then the triad was developed to express moral and spiritual truths, enabling different ideas to be juxtaposed in the most unexpected ways.

Three sisters of lying: perhaps, maybe, guess.

Three sisters of youth: desire, beauty, generosity.

Three sisters of age: contentment, chastity, gentleness.

Three things that bring relief: a servant laying

down his load; a traveller taking off his shoes; a good man approaching death.

Three sources of new life: a woman's belly; a hen's egg; a wrong forgiven.

Three people whose ears are closed: a king bent on conquest; a merchant bent on profit; a monk who thinks himself holy.

Three deaths better than life: the death of a salmon; the death of a robber; the death of an old person at peace with God.

Three vats whose depth no one knows: the vat of a king; the vat of a wealthy bishop; and the vat of a poet's imagination.

Three slender threads on which the world swings: the thin stream of milk from the cow's udder; the thin stalk from which corn springs forth; and the thin string of grace by which God holds us up.

Three dearths that are better than plenty: a dearth of fine words that flatter the proud; a dearth of milch-cows when the grass is scarce; a dearth of friends too fond of beer.

Three clouds that obscure the sight of wisdom: forgetfulness; ignorance; and a little knowledge.

Three elegant things that are best ignored: elegant manners in someone whose heart is false; elegant words from someone who is foolish; elegant prayers from a priest wanting money.

Three signs of rudeness: a visit that lasts longer than the welcome; sharp questions that cut a person's soul; effusive gratitude when none is meant.

Three keys that unlock the secrets of the soul: heavy drinking; violent anger; innocent trust.

A CELTIC PILGRIMAGE

The Celts were, of course, tireless travellers. And I have spent a number of enjoyable holidays retracing their journeys, and visiting the sites associated with the great saints. Places where a saint has lived and prayed have always held a peculiar power over the Christian imagination; and the monasteries of Patrick and Brigid, Columba and Ninian, David and Piran, have attracted countless pilgrims over the centuries. Few of the original buildings remain, many of which were constructed of wood and turf; but even a few shapeless stones, which once formed part of a saint's oratory, possess a strange beauty. There are, to my mind, few happier ways to spend a fortnight than visiting those sites; and there to read the ancient stories and poetry, such as I have collected in this book.

The country richest in Celtic treasures is Ireland, and it is there that I shall start: a fortnight is just sufficient to follow the footsteps of Patrick, Brigid, Kevin, Brendan, Piran and Columba (the latter two in their youth). The sites of Scotland and northern England are more scattered; but a leisurely trip up western Scotland to Iona, and then returning down the eastern side of the country to Northumbria, makes a spectacular route which embraces Ninian, Mungo, the middle-aged Columba, Aidan, Cuthbert and Hilda. The south-west coast of Wales is of course ideal for a children's holiday, with its wide sandy beaches; and on the way there you can pop into Iltut's monastery, and from a base in the Pembroke area you can make excursions in the steps of David and Samson—without too many groans from the back seat. I imagine the

pilgrims—or family of pilgrims—basing themselves at a convenient hotel or hostel, and
going out by car. This is a somewhat unad-
venturous approach, and the more sturdy traveller will prefer walking and camping.

◆IRELAND◆

AROUND BELFAST

Belfast is a more attractive place to stay than
its reputation suggests; but around it are many
pleasant small towns with comfortable hotels
and campsites, of which my favourite is Hills-
borough. You are now in the heart of St. Patrick's country. To the north of Belfast is the
bleak mountain of *Slemish* in County Antrim,
where the young Patrick was enslaved. When
he returned to Ireland, commissioned by the
pope to convert the people to Christianity,
he landed at Strangford Lough, and walked
inland until he found a barn, where he established his first church. This place is now called
Saul, after the Gallic word for barn, *sabhal*;

and on the site now stands a church built in 1932 to commemorate the fifteen-hundredth anniversary of Patrick's arrival. It is in the style of an early Irish church with a round tower. In the churchyard there is an ancient beehive hut in which Celtic monks used to live, suggesting that in the decades following Patrick's mission the monastery was established there. To the east is a hill, *Slieve Patrick*, where he used to go alone to pray; and in 1932 a giant statue of him was erected which is visible for miles across the lush rolling countryside.

To the south-west of Belfast is *Armagh*, a beautiful town filled with eighteenth-century houses of decaying grandeur. It was here that a local chief gave Patrick a hill on which to build his main monastery. Its place is now occupied by the gaunt Protestant cathedral, containing some medieval masonry, but mostly dating from last century. It looks across the town to another hill on which stands the huge Roman Catholic cathedral, also built in the nineteenth century. To me Armagh is a sad, melancholy place, its two cathedrals on opposite hills symbolising the tragedy of a divided Ireland; and Armagh also contains one of the prisons where terrorists are gaoled. Yet both the Catholic and the Protestant churches look back to Patrick as their founder, and both at heart are Celtic in outlook; so perhaps Armagh, where the cathedrals are both dedicated to Patrick, could one day symbolise unity based on a return to common Celtic roots.

A happier place is *Downpatrick*. Here Patrick built his first stone church; and after he died (probably at Saul) his body was taken and buried there. It is also claimed that Brigid and Columba were placed in the same grave. The spot is marked by a large block of granite, with the letters PATRIC inscribed on it; though it looks ancient, it was in fact put there in 1900. Nearby, at the entrance to the grave-yard, is a fine Celtic cross. Downpatrick also contains, incidentally, some stately Georgian houses, and, close to the cathedral, a most handsome school and almshouses built in 1733.

Driving from Belfast to Dublin, just across the border in the Republic, one reaches the town of Dundalk. About a mile before the town there is a right turn to *Faughart*, leading up a steep hill to Brigid's birthplace: a shrine marks the spot beside a stream where, according to legend, the Virgin Mary appeared to the young Brigid, converting her to Christianity.

The journey to Dublin can also take in Kells and Tara, both near the town of Navan. The cathedral at *Kells* is on the site of Columba's most important monastery in Ireland; and the churchyard contains two fine Celtic crosses and an ancient round tower. The famous *Book of Kells*, containing the most stunning Celtic illuminations, was probably made at Iona, and later brought to Kells for safe keeping; it is now to be seen at Trinity College library in Dublin. The earthworks on the hill of *Tara* mark the ancient capital of Ireland; and it is here that Patrick is said to have converted the king by performing magic more powerful than that of the Druids.

From Dublin go south to *Glendalough*, a steep wooded valley with two deep lakes, ringed by mountains. It was on the banks of the lower lake that Kevin first settled, later moving to the upper lake as the bustle of his monastery overwhelmed him; the somewhat dubious remains of his second cell can be seen near the bridge. Near the cathedral is another fine round tower, over a hundred feet high. Incidentally, on the way to Glendalough you can pop in to see the ruins of my own ancestral home, Powerscourt, which, despite a disastrous fire, still boasts a superb Georgian facade and Japanese garden—a monument to the fabulous wealth of the old Irish aristocracy.

Another outing from Dublin is to *Kildare*, the site of Brigid's monastery. Sadly the cathedral there does little to evoke her memory: it dates from the thirteenth century, and its chancel was rebuilt in 1680, having been devastated during battles with the English; and a heavy-handed restoration in 1895 gives the present building a most dark depressing atmosphere. Outside there is a fine medieval round tower, but this too is partly spoiled by the nineteenth-century top which has battlements rather than the traditional cone. Brigid's true memorial, however, is the *Curragh*, to the east of Kildare. It is the largest area of unfenced common land in Ireland, stretching to almost ten square miles, and was cleared by Brigid's monks and nuns. Brigid herself spent many days and nights among her sheep there, and she welcomed local people to graze their livestock alongside hers; and for fifteen centuries no aristocratic landowner has dared to enclose Brigid's pasture.

AROUND DINGLE

Kells is on the route to the next destination; so you may prefer to stay there, or go to Athlone for the night. Just before reaching Athlone there is a left turn to Ballynahown; and then go right to *Clonmacnois*. This is where Piran had his monastery of animals, on the banks of the River Shannon, before going on to Cornwall. In the centuries after Piran's departure it became one of the largest monasteries in Ireland, containing in Norman times twelve churches and a cathedral. The ruins of these buildings are quite spectacular. Also see the rare collection of grave slabs, including some dating back almost to Piran's time.

You now have a complex manoeuvre along remote lanes to visit *Clonfert*, Brendan's monastery. Continue onwards to Shannonbridge; go left to Clonony, Banagher, and left again to Clonfert. The tiny medieval cathedral, with its fine twelfth-century doorway, is in poor repair; and beside it is a track leading to the old bishop's palace, now in ruins. A short distance beyond the palace is a vast area of peat bog, black and smelly. Clonfert is a bleak, desolate place which strangely I find most appealing. To get back on to the main road, you weave through country lanes to Eyrecourt and Portunma.

After the tiring journey, the Dingle peninsula, one of the toes of the south-west foot of Ireland, merits a long leisurely visit. The scenery is as beautiful as anywhere in Ireland; and there are innumerable walks along the cliffs and beaches, and up the mountains. On the north coast of the peninsula is *Mount Brandon*, Ireland's second highest peak, rising straight from the sea. It was here that Brendan spent forty days fasting, during which he conceived his journey across the Atlantic; and at the top of the mountain is a small pile of stones which is said to be the remains of the oratory he built for himself. Near the base of the mountain is *Brandon Bay* where he and his companions constructed their coracle and set sail.

Dingle also contains the *Gallarus Oratory*, the best preserved Celtic building in the whole British Isles. It is rectangular, about twelve feet by eighteen, and built by corbelling, making each stone course of smaller measurement than the one beneath, so the courses eventually meet at the top to form the roof.

While staying on Dingle, drive back to Tralee, and then along the north side of Tralee Bay to *Fenit*, a flat sandy peninsula where Brendan was born. There is no memorial, but one can take a pleasant walk along the coast, looking back across to the mountains of Dingle. A few miles north of Fenit is the small town of *Ardfert* where Brendan first lived as a monk, before moving to Clonfert. Today it contains the ruins of two medieval religious houses, built in Brendan's honour: a Benedictine abbey and a Franciscan priory.

The intrepid pilgrim may also drive from Dingle southwards through Killorglin to either Ballinskelligs or Waterville, where boats can be hired to visit the *Skellig Rocks*. The trip is only possible in calm weather, and even then the Atlantic waves can turn the stomach. Skellig Michael contains an almost complete Celtic monastery, perched on a sheer cliff a hundred feet above the sea: there are six beehive huts and two circular oratories, built by the same method as Gallarus, plus a graveyard. Standing amidst the roar of wind and waves, looking out across the Atlantic, one is overwhelmed by the sheer courage of Brendan and the countless other Celtic seafarers.

From Dingle it is a comparatively easy journey across to Rosslare, and thence the ferry back to Britain. You may make a detour at Tipperary to *Cashel* where Patrick converted King Oengus. A limestone rock where Oengus had his castle rises a hundred feet above the flat plain, and in medieval times a magnificent cathedral was built there, visible for miles around. The town of Cashel, below the rock, is charming, containing some good restaurants—so it is a congenial place to break the journey.

• SCOTLAND AND NORTHERN ENGLAND •

AROUND GLASGOW

The most appropriate place to start is *Whitborn*, on the south-west coast of Scotland. This promontory, surrounded by sea on the east, south and west, is where Ninian founded the first monastery in Britain in 397; it takes its name from the stone church that Ninian built, which was coloured white as a beacon for ships. In Ninian's day it was most easily approached by sea, but today the visitor arrives by road from the north. You reach first the ruins of a medieval priory which now houses an excellent museum containing the earliest memorial stones in Scotland, recording the burial of two members of Ninian's flock. Further on you come to the ruined chapel of St. Ninian: the present stonework dates from the thirteenth century, but beneath are the foundations of an older building, probably used by pilgrims arriving by sea. About a mile around the coast, above the silvery pebble beach, is Ninian's cave, where he is supposed to have gone regularly to pray, and where at the end of his life he lived as a hermit. It contains a number of crosses, dating from the eighth century, carved in the rock.

The route to *Glasgow* across the Galloway Forest path follows Ninian's steps on his main missionary journey. Ninian founded the cemetery where the cathedral now stands; and this in turn became the site of Mungo's monastery. The gaunt medieval cathedral, founded by King David I, is dedicated to Mungo—who has given his name also to an excellent charity caring for down-and-outs.

IONA

Undoubtedly the spiritual centre of the Scottish church is *Iona*, the island off the west coast where Columba founded his great monastery. It is a long, slow, but beautiful drive (or train journey) to Oban, where there are ferries to Mull and Iona. On arrival, instead of following the crowd to the abbey, turn southwards down to the Port of the Coracle on the tip of the island where Columba first landed. From there one can walk up the western shore to Machair where the monks grew their crops; and then back across the island over Eithne's Fold, where the dying Columba bid farewell to his old horse; and finally to the abbey. The buildings which have been so lovingly restored by the modern Iona Community are not Columba's, which were made of wood and straw, but date from the thirteenth-century Benedictine monastery. Before leaving visit the small cove near the jetty called Martyrs

◆   ◆   ◆

◆

Bay, marked now by a war memorial; it was here in 806 that Viking invaders butchered sixty-eight monks, forcing the remainder to abandon Iona and flee to Kells in Ireland— carrying with them their manuscript, now known as the *Book of Kells*.

AROUND LINDISFARNE

The route southwards via Edinburgh seems endless; but this is the journey made by Aidan entirely on foot, on his mission to convert the stubborn Northumbrians.

The trip can be broken by a visit to *Melrose* where Cuthbert first became a monk, and also communed at night with otters. Melrose today is a small town whose houses contain numerous pieces of carved stone, pillaged from the medieval abbey buildings. The abbey ruins themselves still boast some fine stonework, mostly from the late medieval period; but since it found itself in the path of various English invasions of Scotland, and was ransacked by both Robert the Bruce and his English enemies, little survives of any earlier structures. Around Melrose are the hills where Cuthbert tirelessly visited the remote farmsteads, and where he himself grew up and tended sheep.

Lindisfarne is a flat windswept island a few hundred yards from the coast, reached at low tide across a narrow causeway. None of Aidan's monastery remains, though there are the ruins of a later priory, dating from the twelfth century; and in their midst is a modern statue of the gentle saint. The real joy of Lindisfarne is the island itself: as you wander among the sheep and along the rocky shore, you can easily imagine Aidan and Cuthbert making their daily round, visiting the monks and shepherds.

On the mainland opposite Lindisfarne is the ancient capital of Northumbria, *Bamburgh*. It was here that King Oswald, Aidan's patron, had his main castle where he frequently asked the saint to dine. The present Bamburgh castle, like Lindisfarne monastery, is medieval; but, unlike the monastic buildings, it is not a ruin, but was painstakingly restored in the eighteenth century when its owner, Lord Crewe, turned it into a school and infirmary. It is now open to visitors. At the other end of Bamburgh is a pleasant medieval church dedicated to Aidan—the only such dedication in Britain. There is also a museum to Grace Darling, the Victorian heroine who rode out from Farne lighthouse to rescue shipwrecked sailors.

From the fishing town of Seahouses there are regular boats out to the *Farne Islands*. The islands are one of the main nesting grounds for all manner of migratory birds; and thousands of seals sunbathe on the rocks, and bob up and down on the waves. Grace Darling's lighthouse is on the outer island. Cuthbert lived on the inner island, which looks back across to Lindisfarne. Sadly nothing remains of Cuthbert's "city," but in 1370 a small chapel was built in his honour on the site of his enclosure; and also, near the landing-stage, a new guest-house was constructed—a frag-

ment of which still survives—where Benedictine monks continued to offer hospitality as
Cuthbert had done.

AROUND WHITBY

Driving southwards, turn off the main road to
Durham. It is, of course, one of the most magnificent cities in Britain; and the site of the
great cathedral, perched above a bend in the
River Wear, is without equal. This is where
the body of Cuthbert was buried by the
monks fleeing from Viking invasion; and his
tomb is to be found within the cathedral crypt.

Now we can follow the footsteps of the last
great Celtic saint, Hilda. Her first abortive
monastery was on the north bank of the Wear,
although the exact site is unknown. She then
became abbess at *Hartlepool*, where she turned
a small, quiet group of nuns into a major
centre of Christian education. Today a fine
medieval church, dedicated to her, stands on
the tip of the peninsula on the site of her
monastery.

She then moved to *Whitby*, on the Yorkshire coast, where on a high cliff overlooking the grey North Sea she built the largest monastery in Britain. Like Lindisfarne the ruins are of the later medieval abbey, although experts believe some stone from Hilda's buildings may be incorporated within them. It continues to be a popular place of pilgrimage, with groups of students and schoolchildren leaving their coaches a few miles along the coast, and walking above the high cliffs back to the abbey. Next to the ruins is the fascinating parish church, refurnished in the eighteenth century with the best box pews in the country. And the town of Whitby in the valley below is quite charming.

Towards the end of her life Hilda established a daughter-house at *Hackness*, in a beautiful valley a few miles inland from the modern seaside resort of Scarborough, to be a place of quiet retreat. Though seldom visited by the pilgrims who flock to Whitby, the parish church at Hackness contains our closest material link with the great abbess. The chancel arch may date from only a century after her death; and there are the remains of two stone crosses, made by Hilda's nuns at Hackness, one still bearing a head of Christ.

◆ WALES ◆

AROUND GOWER

The energetic pilgrim could take in South Wales on the way back from Ireland. But if you come from the east, you can visit the sites in correct chronological order.

Near the modern resort of Barry, looking across the Bristol Channel, is *Llantwit Major*, where Iltut built his monastery and school. According to legend it was Iltut's monks who constructed the ridge of pebbles across the beach to prevent flooding; today children happily clamber up the ridge, constructing castles at the top. The site of the monastery is now covered by a café and car park; but walking back up the valley, with its flat bottom where Iltut had his farm, you can recapture something of the ancient past. At the top of the valley is the medieval parish church which contains a number of Celtic relics, including the shaft of an eighth-century cross which bears Iltut's name on the back.

Continue along the coast, through Swansea, following the route of Iltut's escape from the bustle of monastic life. When he reached *Oxwich*, on the Gower Peninsula, he concluded he was safe from detection; so he built himself a hut in the woodland on the west side of the bay, where he lived as a hermit for a year. He was eventually discovered, but refused to return to the monastery; so three monks came to look after him. When he died they built a stone oratory, and buried him beneath the floor. This now forms the tiny chancel of a medieval church where, despite its remoteness, services are still held.

AROUND ST. DAVIDS

Iltut was found at Oxwich by a monk travelling to David's monastery, on the western tip of Wales. Although David was a disciple of Iltut, he is regarded as the patron saint of Wales; and the great cathedral on the site of his monastery is the hub of the Welsh church.

David's original community was on what is now a golf course, next to *Whitesand Bay*, a lovely sandy beach. This had been the site of a Roman settlement, Minevia, from which the diocese founded by David took its name. But it proved too exposed to the elements, and too conspicuous to marauders. So they moved a mile inland, to a deep hollow where the cathedral now stands: despite its height only the top of the tower stands above the surrounding land. David's church was built in wood, and the present stone structure dates mainly from the twelfth century. The adjacent bishop's palace, dating from the fourteenth century, boasts a splendid row of arches in alternate yellow and purple stone.

According to legend David was born only a short distance away; and at the moment of his birth a spring of water appeared under the stone where his mother, Non, lay. This spring, which continues to flow, became known as *St. Non's Well*.

About a mile off the coast is *Ramsey Island* where, unbeknown to David, a monk called Jestin arrived by coracle from Brittany to live as a hermit. When local fishermen discovered him and told David, the austere bishop rode out to see him, and asked him to act as his confessor; and from then, until Jestin was killed by pirates, David regularly visited the island to seek counsel. Today in summer there are regular boat trips round the island, which is now a bird sanctuary. Also on the mainland at Porthstinan, two miles west of the cathedral, there are the ruins of a chapel dedicated to Jestin (Justinian) where medieval pilgrims stayed before sailing out to the island.

If you have the energy, it is worth making the journey to *Llandewi-Brevi*, north-east of Lampeter. This is where David conducted his most famous mission: as he preached a mound rose up under his feet, so that he could be seen and heard by the huge crowd that had gathered. He later held a synod on that mound, to which all the priests from his vast diocese came; since he personally had trained them, it must have had the atmosphere of a college reunion. A medieval church stands on the mound, built by Bishop Bec as chapel for a college there. In the churchyard are three Celtic crosses, the middle of which is known as St. David's staff. Set into the north-west exterior wall of the church are two small fragments of the gravestone of Bishop Idnert, a successor to David in the early eighth century.

You should certainly go to Tenby, from where you can take a boat to *Caldy Island*. Here another of Iltut's disciples, Samson, came in 520 to train as a monk, rapidly rising to become abbot; he later went off to Brittany, and founded a new diocese amongst the Celts there at Dol (also worth a visit if you are having a holiday there). There has been a monastery on Caldy almost continuously since Samson, and its monks have been Celtic, Catholic and Anglican in turn; and during this century they have restored the ancient buildings. The oldest is St. David's church, which dates from about two centuries after Samson, and is similar in design to Celtic churches in Ireland. Nearby is the Old Priory, a medieval structure, which contains the famous Ogham stone dating from before Samson's time: it has a double inscription, one in the ancient Ogham language and the other in Latin, bidding those who pass to pray for the soul of Cadoc, the hermit who converted Iltut.

BIBLIOGRAPHY

This is a list of primary sources concerning Celtic Christianity.

Anderson, A. O. and M. O., *Adomnan's Life of St. Columba*, London, 1961.

Bieler, L., *The Patrician Texts in the Book of Armagh*, Dublin, 1979.

Carmichael, A., *Carmina Gadelica*, 2 vols., Edinburgh, 1928.

Clough, S. D. P., *A Gaelic Anthology*, Dublin, 1987.

Colgrave, R., *Two Lives of St. Cuthbert*, Cambridge, 1940.

Doble, G. H., *Lives of the Welsh Saints*, Cardiff, 1971.

* * *

Flower, R. E. W., *Poems and Translations*, London, 1931.

Forbes, A. P., *Lives of St. Ninian and St. Kentigern*, Edinburgh, 1874.

Graves, A. P., *A Celtic Psaltery*, London, 1917.

Greene, D. and O'Connor, F., *A Golden Treasury of Irish Poetry A.D. 600 to 1200*, London, 1967.

Hull, E., *The Poem-book of the Gael*, London, 1912.

Hyde, D., *The Religious Songs of Connacht*, 2 vols., Dublin, 1906.

Jackson, K., *Studies in Early Celtic Poetry*, Cambridge, 1935.

McLean, G. R. D., *Poems of the Western Highlanders*, London, 1961.

Metcalfe, W. M., *Lives of Scottish Saints*, 2 vols., Paisley, 1899.

Meyer, K., *Selections from Ancient Irish Poetry*, London, 1911.

Murphy, G., *Early Irish Lyrics*, Oxford, 1956.

O'Donoghue, D., *St. Brendan the Voyager*, Dublin, 1895.

Rees, W. J., *Lives of the Cambro British Saints*, Llandovery, 1853.

Sharp, E., *Lyra Celtica*, Edinburgh, 1896.

* * *

247

Stevens, J., *Bede's Ecclesiastical History of the English Nation*, London, 1910.

Stokes, W., *Lives of Saints from the Book of Lismore*, Oxford, 1890.

Webb, J. F., *Lives of the Saints*, London, 1965.

DATE